Banished from Eden

Inigo Text Series: 9

Banished from Eden

Original Sin and Evolutionary Theory
in the
Drama of Salvation

Raymund Schwager, SJ

Translated by James Williams

GRACEWING

This work was first published in German in 1997 under the
title *Erbsünde und Heilsdrama: Im Kontext von Evolution,
Gentechnik und Apokalyptik*
by
LIT Verlag, Münster, Germany

This edition published in 2006
by

Gracewing
2 Southern Avenue
Leominster
Herefordshire HR6 0QF

Inigo Enterprises
Links View, Traps Lane
New Malden
Surrey KT3 4RY

*'The expense is reckoned; the enterprise is begun.
It is of God ...'*

ISBN 0 85244 606 3
ISBN 978 0 85244 606 5

Typeset by Action Publishing Technology Ltd,
Gloucester GL1 5SR

Contents

Preface

Raymund Schwager was not only an outstanding popu-
lariser and developer of the ideas of René Girard, he also
played an important role in the original working out of
those ideas. René Girard has always been the first to own
that Raymund Schwager helped him see how he could in
fact modify the pagan sense of sacrifice in order to use it
with an awareness of its uniquely Christian sense. It is
therefore with sadness, as well as with respect and admi-
ration that I for Inigo Enterprises and with Gracewing,
publish this, his last book. It is sad that it *is* his last book
but it is a worthy one written at the height of his creative
powers.

His death was shockingly sudden: only two weeks
before he visited me at Campion Hall, Oxford brimming
with health and energy. He typically spent some of the
precious time in the library checking out English editions
of some of the works referred to in the footnotes of this
book – thorough scholar to the last.

But it is as a friend and Girardian enthusiast that many
of us will miss him most.

William Hewett SJ
Director, Inigo Enterprises

Translator's Foreword

It was with great shock and sadness that friends and colleagues received the news of Raymund Schwager's untimely death in February 2004. Even at the age of sixty-eight he seemed healthy and vigorous, ready to launch into new theological and interfaith projects after his retirement as dean of the theological faculty of the University of Innsbruck. I had enjoyed working with him in the Colloquium on Violence and Religion and in translating other books of his into English: *Jesus in the Drama of Salvation* and *Jesus of Nazareth: How He Understood His Life*. He was an inspiring model of the charitable, holy intellectual.

We had almost finished the work involved in translating *Banished from Eden*. He had yet to give my translation the final reading. For the last stage of the preparation of the manuscript I am indebted to Raymund Schwager's Innsbruck colleagues. Of these I would like to mention especially Nikolaus Wandinger, whose dual fluency in German and English was invaluable in the final reading and correction of the manuscript, and Dietmar Regensburger, who was responsible for the final computer formatting.

As the biblical proverb expresses it, 'The memory of the righteous is for a blessing.' May our brother Raymund, who has fallen asleep in Christ, find light, happiness, and peace in the presence of God with the apostles, martyrs, and all the saints.

James G. Williams

Introduction

There is evil for which human beings are to blame. Conflicts and suffering that stem from this human evil point to it unambiguously. Yet long experience shows that evil cannot be completely overcome in spite of all our efforts. Thus the question: What is the source of this inclination toward conflict and violence and where does evil come from? The faith of Israel fought resolutely to remove it from the good creator God, and so it gradually formed the idea of an original sin which was to make its mark on the whole range of subsequent history : 'You, Adam, what have you done? It was you who sinned, but the fall was not yours alone but reaches to all your descendants!' (4 Ezra 7:118).[1] This Jewish concept influenced early Christianity. In his theology of sin, Paul drew upon rabbinic notions on the one hand, but on the other hand he asserted, against the old pattern of sin stemming from Adam, a new context for salvation in Christ as the new Adam. 'Evidently Paul intended to develop the Adam-Christ parallels in the direction of soteriology and salvation-history in order to make clear the full extent of God's work of salvation based on the death and resurrection of Christ.'[2]

The biblical precedents had further effect in Christian theology and led to the eastern tradition of the doctrine of the 'original calamity'.[3] In the West Augustine explicated the doctrine of original sin in a narrower sense, which would leave a deep imprint on European history for more than a thousand years.[4] In spite of fundamental problems which came with this doctrine, western theology remained true to the heritage of Augustine until the Reformation and beyond. It was first in the Enlightenment that people could no longer conceive of a sin that is inherited. But they also considered other Christian doctrines no longer comprehensible. Modern criticism therefore developed its own dynamics that spared nothing and finally came to an encounter with belief in God and all traditional morality. Criticism reached its high point in Friedrich Nietzsche. He aimed above all at a revaluation of all values. By doing this he intended to free human existence from the dark burden of sin and its accompanying self-destruction and acts of revenge. 'The underdogs, the décadents of every kind, are in revolt against themselves and need victims so as not to loose on themselves their thirst for destruction ... Therefore they have need of an appearance of justice, i.e., a theory, and using this theory they can shift the blame for the fact of their existence, for their being this-or-that, onto some scapegoat.'[5] Nietzsche, in order to overcome this thirst for destruction, criticized the concept of responsibility[6] by which Christianity remains instilled in the blood even of atheists.

> Everywhere that people seek to ascribe responsibility, it has been the instinct for revenge that has sought it. This instinct for revenge became the sovereign of mankind to such an extent that all of metaphysics, psychology, history, and especially morality are marked with it. Just to the extent that humans have engaged in thinking, to that extent the bacillus of revenge has slipped into the content of thought. They have even made God sick with it, they have murdered the innocence of existence in general. How? By reducing every kind of being such-and-such to the will, the intention, and acts of responsibility.[7]

This massive criticism would not be able to change the fact that in the hundred years since Nietzsche the accusations

against and summons to responsibility have only continued. Where people are discontented or suffering they
instinctively seek to find those who are to blame. Faith in
God may diminish and many elements of traditional
morality – in the realm of sexuality, for instance – may
disintegrate, but the concept of responsibility does not
lose its grip. How could it die out, in view of experiences
such as those at Auschwitz, without humans becoming
totally heartless toward one another? The same thing
holds in the private realm. Modern literature and film
never get tired of describing relationships at the point of
breaking in which people excuse themselves and impute
blame to others. The theme of responsibility and guilt
continues to be vital not only in religion and morality but
also in art.[8] Subsequent history refuted Nietzsche.

'To the extent that Humans have engaged in thinking':
so Nietzsche stated, and to the extent that people today
engage in thinking they cannot bypass the concept of
responsibility; they are constantly tempted to accuse
others for evil that is suffered. And yet it is accusation that
creates new evil, which leads to further counter-charges.
Modern criticism could call in question the concept of sin
but it could change nothing of the massive experiences
that led to this concept. We find above all the total self-
exculpation that originates in total self-accusation, as F.
Dürrenmatt expresses it:

> In the wasteland of our century, in this last tango of the
> white race, no one is guilty and no one is responsible
> any more. No one can do anything about it and no one
> has intended it. It actually continues without anyone.
> Everyone is carried along by the current and caught in
> some grating. We are too collectively guilty, too collec-
> tively imbedded in the sins of our fathers and forefa-
> thers. We are mere grandchildren. That is our bad luck,
> not our fault.[9]

So, according to Dürrenmatt, we are collectively totally
guilty and thus simultaneously innocent. Isn't this

paradox reminiscent of the traditional doctrine of original sin?

Actually, even authors today who no longer understand themselves as Christians detect a profound insight in the doctrine of original sin. N. Luhmann makes the judgement that 'The dogma of original sin was a schema of self-observation unequalled and unsurpassed historically. It led, if not on the psychological then at least on the communicative level, to moral self-condemnation and therewith to a mitigation of moral criticism.'[10] M. Horkheimer goes even further in an interview published under the title, 'Longing for the Wholly Other'. He says,

> The most magnificent teaching in both religions, both the Jewish and the Christian, is – I call to mind here a phrase of Schopenhauer's – the doctrine of original sin. It has determined history to this point and currently defines the world for thinking people. It is possible only under the presupposition that God created mankind with a free will.[11]

The interviewer asked whether Horkheimer shared the view of Schophauer. He answered, 'On this point I am also an adherent of Schopenhauer. I believe also that the doctrine of original sin is one of the most significant theories in religion.'[12]

Although there are those in the modern context who understand and appreciate the idea of original sin, this doctrine causes great difficulties today for many Christians and theologians. The greatest difficulty lies in the notion of hereditary transmission of sin, even if one emphasizes that here the concept 'sin' is to be understood by analogy. All of modern thinking is grounded in the distinction, indeed the separation, between two great realms of reality: the *res extensa* and the *res cogitans* (Descartes), or nature and freedom (Kant). In view of this separation, with all its methodological consequences, many see in the concept 'original sin' a confusion of questions and categories. A concept belonging to nature (hereditary transmission), becomes mythically confused with one that is to be ascribed to the realm of freedom (sin). P. Ricoeur says, for example, 'Speculation on the transmission of a sin issuing from a first man is a later rationalization that mixes ethical categories with biological ones.'[13] For this reason numerous theologians have dropped the teaching of an historical fall and the inheritance of sin.[14] In a paper on the main types of original sin in modern theology S. Wiedenhofer traces the majority of the models back to unclarified presuppositions, and he holds that one must choose between two ways. Either we accept 'that there are, in the course of European thought, fundamental differentiations which we may not go behind', or we begin 'from a complementary multiplicity of possible ways of knowing, and so in this context we assume a specific rationality and necessity of mythical thinking'. In the latter case 'even the 'mythical' elements of the doctrine of original sin' would maintain 'a theoretical value'.[15] Do we actually stand before this choice, of either accepting the differentiations of modern thought as something we cannot go behind, or of remaining bound to a mythical form of thinking?

Precisely one of the most central modern differentiations, the separation between nature and freedom, is one the development of the sciences has called at least partially into question. So, for example, evolutionary theories of knowledge and sociobiology attempt to clarify human knowledge and behaviour from the standpoint of natural history. Even if much remains very problematic in this attempt, such projects should not be rejected en masse. For instance, K. Lorenz ventures the 'search for a natural history of human knowledge',[16] on the one hand, while on the other he speaks of the mortal sins of civilized humanity and the '... monstrous evolutionary paths leading to catastrophes'.[17] As requisite for an authentically human culture he maintains that 'It is the prerequisite of all civilized communal life that people learn to control their impulses.'[18] Whoever speaks of the need to curb instincts in spite of the attempt to write a natural history of human knowledge, must hold fast to freedom.

Other phenomena in today's world also point in a similar direction. H. Arendt saw already some decades ago an utterly new form of interpenetration of nature and freedom in the atom bomb, and she came to the conviction that the 'distinction between nature and history, which dominated our thinking for so long, ... is now a thing of the past'.[19] Also more recent studies of the history of the natural sciences (Th. Kuhn, I. Lakatos, et al) are more and more inclined to loosen the distinction between nature and history, and modern scientific studies elaborate the intellectual connection between researchers who were previously associated with quite different realms.[20] In this respect the works of B. Latour are especially informative. He shows the dual imagery of modern thinkers and artists through a manifold analysis. The strict separation of nature from history and society belongs to the theoretical claim, or 'constitution', of these moderns. But their practice appears completely different, for they produce hybrids, as Latour names them, namely images that belong inseparably to nature, to history, and to society.[21] Latour concludes that we have never been 'modern'.[22] By that he does not want to deny that the theoretical claim modernity made for itself in recent centuries was very effective. The relationship between nature and human history since the Enlightenment and the beginnings of the natural sciences has actually become more complex, but a real and complete separation between them never occurred. It is precisely the theoretical demand for separation that in practical ways provoked a completely new and far more intensive cooperation than earlier on.

This new situation produced consequences for thought that J.P. Dupuy makes clear in his analysis of concealed conceptual models in very diverse fields of study (biology, cybernetics, economics, sociology, political science, psychology, etc.).[23] He shows that isomorphic structures of thought have developed through research procedures in quite different areas of knowledge. Integral to these structures is that certain constants, e.g., the particular and the universal, the accidental and the regular (man and nature), are no longer viewed as isolated and in opposition, but are bound together through 'tangled hierarchies' ('hierarchies enchevetrées'). Every view of objects and nature presupposes a quite definite subjective standpoint that enters into the result of the observation either directly or in a concealed manner.[24] Even the laws of nature obtain a new meaning,[25] for it becomes evident that they stand in connection with the human action whose intention is to dominate nature and constrain it to produce answers. The idea of autonomy also, which in past centuries meant primarily control (over objects, nature, and oneself), obtains in this context a changed sense and is now to be understood chiefly as reciprocal dependence.[26]

These brief references obviously do not intend to offer a comprehensive overview of recent thinking. Certainly they neither suffice as a survey of the problematic of nature and freedom in all their complexity. They may, however, make clear that one must be careful about accepting unbridgeable differentiations. For a theology intending to be modern and therefore adhering to such presuppositions could turn out to be bound to antiquated ideas from the seventeenth to the nineteenth centuries. It is at least possible that the truth of the matter is just to the contrary and that the concept *original sin*, which ostensibly confuses separate realms in a mythological way, preserves a deeper and critical synopsis of what the 'dogma' of modernity has on the surface artificially separated.

Since the presuppositions for a contemporary doctrine of original sin are not at all clear, it is impossible to sketch a rigorously systematic doctrine. We have rather to deal carefully with different points of departure in which three perspectives in particular are to be distinguished. We can observe the experience of suffering and of evil both in the context of natural and human history as well as in the context of supernatural history.[27] These three standpoints or levels can obviously never be separated but are nonetheless distinguishable for purposes of thought. The following three chapters take up these three perspectives.

In the first chapter human history is in the foreground, in the second natural history (evolution), and in the third supernatural history. In the fourth chapter I will attempt a more systematic confrontation with the modern world view. Since the question of evil includes also the devil or Satan, the last chapter is devoted to this question, and I will ask how this theme is related to original sin.

The first two chapters were published previously as articles.[28] They are here incorporated unchanged, with the exception of the method of citing in the footnotes, so the reader will be able to follow the development of the argument. This produces a few small repetitions. However these repetitions correspond to the movement of thought that proceeds step by step and that is necessary, given the recurring aspects of the questions we are pursuing. Since many key questions are open for investigation, we must illuminate these in multiple ways and from different sides in order to press toward answers that have the capacity to persuade through their inner coherence.[29] An earlier publication also underlies the last chapter about the devil or Satan. However, this text was partially reworked to make clearer its connection with the doctrine of original sin and the modern view of the world. I have developed my reflections here on evil in the context of a salvation history that is understood dramatically.[30]

Notes

1   Cf. Also 4 Ezra 3:21, 26; 7:116.
2   K. Kertelge, 'Adam und Christus: Die Sünde Adams im Lichte der Erlösungstat Christi nach Röm 5:12–2', in *Anfänge der Christologie*, 141–153.
3   Cf. Hauke, *Heilsverlust in Adam*.
4   Cf. Delameau, *Le péché et la peur*.
5   Nietzsche, 'Erlösung von aller Schuld', in *Werke* III, 821.
6   *Tr. Note: The German word is *Verantwortung*. As a noun and a verb it may mean accountability or obligation. As in English it may also be used in expressions like shifting responsibility or denying one's accountability. Recognizing this is important in understanding Nietzsche, who advocated an existence without self-justification.
7   Nietzsche, 'Erlösung von aller Schuld', in *Werke* III, 822.

8 Cf. K.J. Kuschel, 'Schuld as Thema der Gegenwartsliteratur', *Orientierung* 50 (1986), 175–180; 195–197; 206–209.
9 Dürrenmatt, 'Theaterprobleme', in idem, *Theaterschriften und Reden*, 122.
10 Luhmann, *Ecological Communication*, 123.
11 Horkheimer, *Die Sehnsucht nach dem ganz Anderen*, 64–65.
12 Ibid., 65.
13 Ricoeur, *The Problem of Evil*, 83.
14 Cf. The comprehensive presentation by U. Baumann, *Erbsünde?*
15 Wiedenhofer, *Hauptformen gegenwärtiger Erbsündentheologie*, 327f.
16 Lorenz, *Die Rückseite des Spiegels*.
17 Lorenz, *Civilized Man's Eight Deady Sins*, 18.
18 Ibid., 55.
19 Arendt, *Fragwürdige Traditionbestände*, 69.
20 Cf., e.g., Sharpin and Schaffer, *Leviathan and the Air-Pump*.
21 For example, plants and foodstuff changed by genetic technology, living creatures from artificial fertilization, changes in the environment (holes in the ozone layer, etc.). In this regard the cooperation between mankind and nature had already begun a long time ago – at least since the neolithic revolution (cultivation of plants and animals).
22 Latour, *Wir sind nie modern gewesen*.
23 Dupuy, *Ordres et Désordres*; idem, *La panique*; idem, 'The Self-Deconstruction of the Liberal Order'; idem, 'Tangled Hierarchies'; idem, 'Totalization and Misrecognition', in *Violence and Truth*, 75–100.
24 'The arbitrariness of the point of view is unsurpassable: we see it in the way in which the meta-level is relative to the boundaries of the subject; it depends on it, while the extent of the latter, what it encompasses, is largely left to the discretion of the observer. Science is necessarily arbitrary since it rests upon hypothesis, a point of departure always starting from a specific place but still absolute within this locality.' Dupuy, *Ordres et désordres*, 244–245.
25 'The laws of nature are no longer what they seemed to be in the past … Fallen from their superior place of reason that preserved them from all contamination at the level of actual events, the laws as we think them now are as much the product of phenomena as the phenomena are the effect of the laws. Thus the works of nature begin to draw nearer to human deeds.' Ibid., 224.
26 'If it is difficult for us to think the distinction between autonomy and control, it's because we remain prisoners of the dualism established by the dominant paradigm in the West: the subject, consciousness, self-mastery, mind and knowledge on the one side; the world of objects, of reality in-itself, matter, the inanimate on the other.' Ibid., 133. – When we make a precise comparison of different fields of science, the present situation certainly turns out to be very contradictory, indeed absurd, as Dupuy makes clear in his analysis of Derrida's thought: 'It so happens that the highly complex figures of self-deconstruction and of deconstruction that I have tried to analyse were familiar to me long before I became interested in the philosophy of Derrida. I encountered them in two domains completely different from this one, where they had a radi-

cally opposite meaning. The first was in the theory of self-organizing systems (cf. Atlan), and the second was in the anthropology of Louis Dumont. In both of these, tangled hierarchy – as the reversal of a hierarchy within itself – is treated as autonomy. Whereas, for deconstruction, a tangled hierarchy is supposed to indicate the impossibility of achieving autonomy or self-sufficiency of any kind ... Thus we seem doomed to continue in this absurd situation, where the same form is seen by some as representing autonomous totality, and is used by others to deconstruct any pretension to autonomy and totalization.' Dupuy, 'Self-Deconstruction', 14.

27 Cf. Fessard, *L'Historie et ses trois niveaux d'historicité.*
28 Schwager, 'Neues und Altes zur Lehre von der Erbsünde' (chapter 1 of this book); idem., 'Evolution, Erbsünde und Erlösung'.
29 On the theoretical background see Schwager, et al, 'Dramatische Theologie als Forschungsprogramm'.
30 C.f. Schwager, *Jesus in the Drama of Salvation; Dramatische Erlösungslehre,* ed. J. Niewiadomski, et al.

Chapter 1

The Primal History in a New Light

In his overview of the current theological discussion of original sin, S. Wiedenhofer refers to numerous problem areas that require further clarification in spite of positive contributions to them. These include questions about the history of dogma and exegesis, as well as the relation of theology to secular fields of study (anthropology, history of religion, cosmology, etc.).[1] But beyond all particular questions, the 'fundamental systematic theological problem of the doctrine of original sin' for current theology lies in 'how to express simultaneously the universality of original sin (i.e., its necessity) and its attribution of guilt to humankind. The entire recent discussion revolves in effect around this question.'[2] In this contribution I cannot deal exhaustively with all the questions up for discussion. My intention is rather to sketch a proposal for discussion that seeks to bring together both new and old approaches in a constructive manner.

The Dynamics and Universality of Sin

Wiedenhofer counts E. Drewermann's *Strukturen des Bösen* [Structures of Evil],[3] together with Paul Ricoeur's *Symbolik des Bösen* [Symbolism of Evil],[4] as the 'two most important contributions to the contemporary theology of original sin'.[5] Drewermann actually goes quite fully into the Yahwist primal history and treats it from exegetical, psychoanalytic, and philosophical viewpoints. In the exegetical part he analyses the Garden narrative and shows that for the Yahwist sin has its origin in anxiety; then he interprets the entire Yahwist primal history as an explication of the inner dynamics of this sin. Drewermann finds the decisive proof for the theme of anxiety in Eve's answer to the serpent. To be sure, the woman initially corrects the seductive voice's exaggeration of what the Lord God said, but in doing so she herself falls into exaggeration ('you may not touch it' [Gen. 3:3]). To interpret this reaction Drewermann refers back to the 'basic psychological knowledge' that 'a command must be sharpened when there is a growing inclination to transgress it'.[6] Through the question of the serpent, who deceptively changes the meaning of what God said, a slumbering possibility awakens in the woman. 'On the one hand the wish stirs in her to act against the prohibition of God; ... On the other hand the threat of the death sentence (2:17b) is acute and compels the woman to reject her wish. It is the first time that the death threat from God fills the woman with anxiety. And she reacts accordingly.'[7] Anxiety forms in the woman because she tries to remain faithful to God, while God himself becomes an object of deadly menace to her. Since the serpent reinforces this feeling that it first deceptively awakened, she falls into its power spontaneously. The woman's lapse stemming from anxiety looks to Drewermann like the appearance of inevitability,[8] and the punishment is that 'man falls back into what he is without God'.[9]

The further transgressions originate in 'what Adam and Eve have done. Cain is the child of Adam and Eve not only genealogically, but also theologically.'[10] Cain, the founder of the first city, is able to live because God protects him through the injunction of sevenfold revenge against anyone who slays him. But even this dramatic measure is not enough to check evil in the world. With Lamech and his sons both the works of civilization and alienation from God increase.[11] Thus the sevenfold revenge becomes the totally boundless seventy-sevenfold.[12]

Drewermann interprets the further narration of the sons of God and daughters of men chiefly in the framework of fertility cults. At the same time, however, he finds in the primal history

that J [the Yahwist] shows how God responds each time to a human mis-step by trying to limit its negative consequences, but every time humans transgress these limitations immediately afterwards: the clothing with skins (3:21) is followed by the story of fratricide (4:2ff.); the divine prerogative of blood vengeance (4:15) is followed by the song of Lamech (4:23–24). As a further reduction and softening of the consequences that God's 'preventive measure' imposes we would point out also in Genesis 4:25–26 the compensation God creates through the fertility that he has given to the human race [the conception and birth of Seth]. So it is absolutely appropriate to the prevailing logic of the narrative that the consequent counter-move humans make against God's preventive measure takes up the theme of fertility and turns the wrong way into rebellion. Something similar continues also in 8:21–22 [divine promise never again to destroy the earth] and 9:20–27 [Noah's cursing of Canaan]: the fertility of the land that God guarantees after the flood becomes the occasion of errors, which result in severe consequences. Noah's blessing leads into the table of nations (Genesis 10), but with that it leads also to the conflict that men wanted to 'solve' in building the Tower of Babel (Gen. 11:1–9). The result, however, is that they make conflict finally global and unsolvable.[13]

In the flood narrative Drewermann finds a historicizing of cultic narratives from the cosmic cyclical return into chaos and its renewal. The world before the flood being shown as filled with violence indicates how immeasurable sin had become. As the Yahwist – referring to Drewermann – thinks radically of evil, giving 'a radical answer based on God's compassion: on all human beings and on

all human deeds God must have compassion, for otherwise only total destruction would occur'.[14] God's kindness
is particularly clear in his choosing of Noah, who is not
described as having special virtue; then after the flood he
promises Noah never again to destroy the earth, even
though the desires of men are 'evil from the beginning'
(Gen. 8:21). Corresponding to these evil desires and
deeds the subsequent history appears as 'a development
of the scattering and confusion (Gen. 11:9) that establishes
history as we know it now'.[15]

The knowledge of good and evil is a central theme of the
whole Yahwist primal history, for 'what God created as
good and what is good in his sight, is changed into something negative when the communion with God is broken';
the consequences of sin then have a 'peculiar inevitability.'[16] However, according to Drewermann, the 'series of
events exhibits' some 'theological gaps'.[17] In order to fill
the gaps and to convey the logical consistency of the
Yahwist's interpretation to a modern understanding,
Drewermann attempts a broader interpretation in a
second work, which combines mythological and depth-
psychological approaches. He moves from the present text
back to the earlier myths showing through it, and he
deduces from it a depth-psychological interpretation. In
this interpretation he holds that all the essential steps of
libido development may be found in the Yahwist primal
history, a 'history of development, complete in itself,
between birth and maturity'.[18] The Yahwist presents this
process – according to Drewermann – as a total history of
fault, which corresponds to the modern medical idea of
neurosis.

If Drewermann's exegesis[19] is somewhat convincing,
his psychoanalytic interpretation operates by means of
associations difficult to control. The set of problems in
human and social life that Drewermann expounds in the
exegetical section is thereby reduced to an individual
psychology in which, inter alia, the massive theme of
murder is rendered harmless as mere aggressive tendencies. Whether transposing the principle that 'ontogeny

recapitulates phylogeny'[20] may be meaningful and justified, must remain open here. Let us, however, pursue the
question whether the inner dynamics of the primal history
can today be interpreted understandably without a detour
by way of putative myths and with a much closer reading
of the present biblical text. And here I refer to the text as a
whole, not just to the reconstructed (and thus problematic)
Yahwist.

I propose an experimental approach to this question by
way of René Girard's mimetic theory. According to
Girard's anthropology, imitation of others precedes reflective knowledge and operates with a 'quasi-osmotic immediacy'[21] in aspiring toward a model [mimesis]. If this
desire is oriented to a limited object, then the imitator is
caught without fail in a rivalrous relationship with his or
her model, because the imitator strives to obtain the same
particular object as the model. But the model soon begins
also to imitate the imitation of his or her 'disciple', and in
this process both become doubles or 'enemy brothers'.
Their rivalry can easily grow into open aggression, even
into homicide. In the wake of imitation [mimesis] evil
spreads further like contagion, for it draws still other
people and all realms of life – even reason – into its
domain. Girard holds, however, that there is a self-limita-
tion in violence, for in the operation of the mimesis that
creates the problem the reciprocal aggression can
suddenly turn into the act of all against one. The others,
the all, will transfer upon this single person [scapegoat] all
their aggressions and projections. They will attribute to
this victim both blame for the outbreak of violence and
credit for the sudden and seemingly wonderful return of
peace. They are not aware of the reason for this 'miraculous' return, which occurs because of the unperceived
working of the scapegoat mechanism. The passive and
accidental victim is thus sacralized, yet also exalted to the
status of an active, divine and heroic figure. The originally
spontaneous and violent immolation is, on the one hand,
instinctively repeated in ritual acts of sacrifice so as to
renew, as much as possible, its effect of mediating peace.

On the other hand, it is the origin of sacral prohibitions and taboos, which attempt to restrain dangerous imitation. Other institutions finally develop out of ritual sacrifices, as, for instance, sacred kingship and the city.

It is immediately striking that essential elements of this mimetic theory are present in the biblical primal history. Sin begins with a counterfeit imitation of God that engenders rivalry. The latter is extended as rivalry between brothers and reaches its first climactic point as murder. The sevenfold vengeance on anyone who might kill Cain increases to seventy-sevenfold, and so before the great flood the entire world is full of violence. Likewise the relation of the genders and sexuality are drawn into the dynamics of this rivalry (Gen. 3:7, 16; 4:23f.; 6:1–3; 9:21f.). From the start we see the tendency, as in the scapegoat mechanism, to blame others for evil [Adam, Eve, Cain], and the narrative mentions for the first time religious and cultural institutions [ritual sacrifice, sacred norms, the city] in connection with violence. Finally there are also various forms of mythologizing tendencies [the sons of God, giants, etc.]. There is only one key theme of Girard's theory which is not directly addressed anywhere in the biblical primal history: collective ganging up on an accidental victim. Yet the omission of this element is not a decisive objection against the mimetic theory as an interpretive hypothesis, for the missing theme is found in other Old Testament passages.

Like Drewermann, Girard also holds that belief in Yahweh grew out of an ancient sacral tradition in which the transmitted myths were gradually transformed in the light of new experiences of God.[22] According to Girard, however, myths are narratives which conceal what is most important. Unlike Drewermann, in interpreting the Old Testament he doesn't refer back to the world of the sacred that can be reconstructed behind the biblical text. Rather, he aims at the full disclosure of its mythical remnants. This occurs in other Old Testament texts, but definitively in the New Testament.[23] Therefore the biblical primal history alone does not suffice for Girardian interpretation, which must bring the entire Bible into its purview. But as soon as this happens, the theme of collective violence shows up in multiple ways. In the prophetic writings we frequently find descriptions of how people come together in a menacing fashion against the messenger of Yahweh. The same thing is reported of gentile peoples who band together against Israel. But above all, many evildoers lie in ambush against a single, solitary righteous person. In numerous psalms of lament and complaint the worshipper almost always sees himself surrounded by deceitful enemies who are trying to take his life.[24] So all the important elements of the mimetic theory are found in the Old Testament. If we draw upon it subsequently for a more precise interpretation of the biblical primal history, we will thus – by contrast to a psychoanalytic interpretation – not be introducing a perspective foreign to the subject under study.

In Genesis 3 the serpent begins its seductive speech not with a statement of its own, but by deceptively imitating what God has said previously: 'Did God really tell you not to eat from any of the trees of the garden?' (3:1).This is an attempt to imitate God from the very start, but it focuses exclusively on a single aspect of what he said ('you shall not eat'); through the serpent's misuse of the prohibition the semblance of a perverse idol is produced. The woman responds to the narrow and deceptive imitation by initially making a correction, but then falling herself into a restriction of what God said. As a counter-move the serpent explicitly negates a word of God that the woman reports, and instead it places before her eyes the possibility of a direct and full imitation of God ('you will be as God and know good and evil') by means of eating the forbidden fruit. Therefore the garden narrative comprises a complex mimetic interplay. This drama leads from the deceptive imitation of a word from God, through the negation of another divine word, to the direct imitation of that perverse image of God that is produced in this drama.

Whether or not the woman falls into a certain exaggeration in the mimetic interplay out of repressed anxiety, as Drewermann argues, cannot be immediately determined from the text. What is certain, however, is that the biblical narrative does not see this as the immediate cause of the fall, for the woman eats because she sees that the tree was 'good for food, pleasing to the eyes, and desirable for gaining wisdom' (Gen. 3:6). Although the tree was already there, it acquires for Eve a tempting aspect only after the exchange with the serpent. What seduces Eve is not the fruit as such but the fruit the serpent designates as desirable. In doing so, the seductive voice feigns to accept God as worthy of imitation, whereas in truth it is itself an aping of God in order to convey upon itself the appearance of being a model worthy of imitation. The serpent consequently proves to be a symbol of that mimesis which falls into immediate desire through an imitation that is too restrictive.[25] According to the biblical narrative this mimesis leads to the Fall, while anxiety is explicitly mentioned only after the transgression (Gen. 3:10f.). Many other texts in the Old Testament confirm this, for the apostasy of Israel from Yahweh is very often described as the imitation of the abominations of other peoples or as running after foreign gods.[26]

The mimetic theory holds that multiple forms of rivalry stem from acquisitive imitation. This is precisely what one finds in the primal history. On the one hand God, as held up for imitation by the serpent, appears as a rival of human beings. Yet on the other hand the fall leads immediately to disturbed relations among humans (experience of nakedness, the man ruling over the woman) and to perversion of the relation of mankind and nature [deadly rivalry between the woman and the serpent, the man's heavy toil with the soil[27]]. That God does not directly punish Adam and Eve with death certainly does not mean in this context that he has set aside or withdrawn the threatened punishment.[28] Rather, how punishment and death follow from sin will be concretely narrated through the theme of rivalry.

The narrative of fratricide is far more than an appendage to the Eden story. It has, on the one hand, the character of an origin narrative in its own right, for it recounts the beginning of the practice of blood revenge, the founding of the first city, and the first sacrifices. On the other hand, it coheres seamlessly with the garden narrative through the theme of rivalry and death.[29] We see that the death God has threatened as a consequence of the transgression becomes a concrete reality in Abel's death at the hands of his brother. So punishment, from the standpoint of the primal history, is not a measure taken by God which comes from without, but is an inner consequence of an evil deed. This is a consequence that can befall a person who is not directly guilty, but who nonetheless stands in close relationship to the guilty party. Whoever falls into covetous imitation is immediately seduced into a rivalry that easily grows in various ways into a violent act.[30] The inner consequence of these mimetic dynamics in no way entails an absolute necessity, for Eve is able, at least at first, to resist the serpent. Also, after rivalry is fully awakened in Cain, God himself addresses him and tells him to become once more the master of the sin lying in wait.[31] Although there is, therefore, no necessity to commit sin, the latter obtains its full form on account of the inner consequence of covetous imitation, and this mimetic force is simultaneously the process of punishment. God does not slay evil-doers with his own hand but he delivers them over to their own deeds, which lead with severe consistency to sorrowful dispute in social relations and to violent death.[32] The death of all humans is to be seen in light of the death of Abel, who dies as the first man, and because of this real death in a world of anxiety and violence is shown to be a consequence of sin.

The forces at play in violence as the primal history represents them appear even more clearly if one observes the founding character of the narration of fratricide. Cain is the first builder of a city [to which sacral kingship also belongs[33]], and the sacral institution of blood revenge comes about for the first time by means of the sign God places on him. Cain and Abel are also the first to be presented as sacrificers. Thus we find the three primary religio-cultural institutions that, according to the mimetic theory, stem from the founding murder and that work [if only precariously] against the universal tendency to violence. The biblical primal history indicates the origin of these institutions in a violent event, but it particularly emphasizes how endangered cultural accomplishment are and how sin can once again find new nourishment in them.The blood revenge introduced for Cain's protection degenerates with Lamech to unlimited vengeance, and the city [with its accompanying sacral kingship] becomes finally, in the narrative of the Tower of Babel, the place of the greatest rivalry of humans with God as they attempt to build a tower all the way up to heaven.

Consequently, the story of fratricide does not simply relate an individual archetypical event. Rather, through the three religio-cultural institutions it develops the story of how the evil involved in transgressing God's command exceeds these opposing cultural forces and dominates them.[34] So it is that a punishment weighs upon all human culture and society according to the primal history. The consequences of sin show therefore with even greater clarity that God did not want to withhold something good from humans when he forbade them to eat from the tree of the knowledge of good and evil (Gen. 2:17); his intention was rather to spare them the experience of evil.[35]

If the narrative of Cain and Abel has a founding character, then there is yet another aspect to observe, as J. Williams indicates. When God asks Cain where his brother is, he answers, 'I do not know' (Gen. 4:9). Exegetes usually see in this answer only Cain's attempt to conceal his individual guilt. But if Cain is a founding figure in sacred cultural institutions, then the attempt to cover up his deed says something pertinent to these institutions. In them also a tendency to concealment must be at work. Williams' comment may therefore be correct: 'Cain's denial of knowledge about what happened to his brother could be construed as a universal ritual phenomenon.'[36] Hence a primordial lie is given with the primordial murder. These are two themes that are interrelated in the whole Bible. Just as violence rules by means of the sacred institutions, so also a process of concealment is at work in them.[37]

Girard, in order to show the full distinctiveness of the biblical narration of the founding murder, compares it to the founding myth of Rome,[38] in which the three essential elements are the same. There also we find two brothers in rivalry. One of them murders the other, and this murderer is the founder of the city. It is exactly these points of agreement that also highlight the decisive difference between the Roman myth and the biblical narrative. Rome sees itself in continuity with Romulus, the slayer and the founder of the city. Yahweh, however, the one to whom Israel appeals, takes a stand for Abel and heeds his blood, which cries out from the ground to heaven (Gen. 4:10). In other biblical accounts too Yahweh is no longer a sacral divinity through whom humans glorify or conceal their violent acts, even though much in the Old Testament remains ambiguous in this respect. Yahweh shows again and again in decisive moments that he is a compassionate God who hears the cries of victims.[39]

In the further course of the primal history the flood prologues are especially worthy of note. R. Oberforcher even attributes a 'key compositional position' to them.[40] The dramatic action between God and humans really reaches a high point here, for the wickedness of men increases on the earth to such an extent (Gen. 6:5) that evil obtains a global dimension: 'But the earth was corrupt in the eyes of God and full of violence' (Gen. 6:11). Here it is no longer simply a matter of human corruption, but the corruption of the earth in general is precisely formulated.[41] A specific concept of sin (Hebrew *chamas*) is used in combination with other formulas 'for a total assertion of offence against God'.[42] Indeed, in this narrative statement about sin, violence appears as the essence of evil. This universal corruption includes also the animals, 'for all creatures of flesh lived in corruption on the earth' (Gen. 6:12), although the text does not indicate how this corruption spread to the animal world.

An expansion of evil to other creatures is found also in

the narrative immediately preceding the flood myth. In it the sons of God have intercourse with the daughters of men. Oberforcher may therefore be right when he speaks of an expansion of evil 'into a general context of humans and creation' in connection with the flood story.[43] God's reaction to the new extent of evil is therefore different from what it was before. He announces not simply further punishment, but he reconsiders creation, although he had judged it as good in the beginning. Indeed, God himself is affected: 'He regretted that he had made mankind on the earth, and his heart was grieved' (6:6). This 'grief' of God is the origin of the decision to destroy both humans and animals – a decision that was immediately limited in that one man (with his family) found favour before God, and through him the human race and the animal species continued on earth. Yet how?

The biblical text says that before the flood every device the human heart conceived was 'always only evil' (Gen. 6:5), and immediately again after the flood it states that human aspirations were 'evil from youth on' (Gen. 8:21).[44] Wickedness is seen also right away and concretely in Ham's offence concerning his father Noah. Because of this Noah curses him (9:18–25), and even the descendants of Shem must suffer evil, although no precise guilt is ascribed to them: another people will dwell among their tents (Gen. 9:27). The manifold posterity of Noah leads then directly to the attempt of men, presumptuously and in rivalry with God, to preserve their unity (the tower up to heaven), an attempt that ends finally in confusion and dispersion.

So what does the primal history intend to teach in the narrative of the flood if the subsequent world is not better? The answer to this difficult question is made even more difficult by the fact that the narrator here works quite remarkably with mythical elements [sons of God who marry human women; a flood that covers the whole earth; an ark spacious enough to accommodate pairs of all animals on earth]. We find hints pointing toward an answer only if we observe closely what God says after the flood and compare this with his words before the flood: 'I will never again curse the earth because of mankind; for the desires of man's heart are evil from his youth on' (Gen. 8:21). The continuous malice of human beings is given here as the reason why God will never again curse and destroy the earth. Before the flood, however, this malice was the reason for God's resolve to devote all flesh to destruction. So the texts give exactly the same reason for two completely opposed divine reactions. One can only draw the conclusion that the flood story intends, on the one hand, to highlight a dimension of evil which would be sufficient reason in itself to render null and void the entire created order of human and animal worlds. On the other hand, it articulates a promise that in no way depends any longer on the behaviour of humans (and animals). Although God saw in the beginning that everything was good, future history rests no longer on the intrinsic goodness of what was created, but solely on God's promise, which he gives in clear awareness of human evil.

For the question of original sin under investigation here we have thus advanced to an initial significant result. Sin begins in the paradise story with imitative desire and leads through different forms of rivalry to violence [fratricide]. So it is that it attains such a universal extent in the flood narrative that it even calls in question the whole created order. Traditional theology placed the question of original sin only in the context of the garden story, thus it was real progress when theology also began to pay express attention to the story of Cain and Abel. Still, however, the flood story was almost completely overlooked. Yet it is first in this narrative, as Oberforcher makes clear, that the connection between a universal expansion of violence and the order of creation is addressed and thereby an essential question concerning original sin is raised. This is sin experienced as so universal that it even seems to affect the entire creation; it can no longer be construed as the offence of an individual and so raises the question of hereditary transmission.

Is it possible to gather still more precise details from the flood narrative about the general context of evil for humans and the created order? This is difficult regarding the cosmic dimension, because the narrator uses mythical language for the statements about the sons of God and the animals, a language that does not permit knowing how and where one may speak of moral evil. Concerning the general human context, however, the mimetic theory allows us at least to sketch an interpretive hypothesis. By the concept of the sacrificial crisis Girard paraphrases the contagious spread of aggression in the wake of imitation or 'mimesis' in which those affected are possessed by monstrous imaginations. This crisis undergoes an abrupt resolution when the reciprocal acts of aggression converge in the act of all against one person. Essential elements of this scenario are clearly present in the flood narrative. This crisis begins with monstrous imaginations (coupling of the sons of God with the daughters of men) and then plays itself out in a world full of violence. It reaches a point of polarization between one person and all the others. The great difference from the typical mythical account is that in the flood story the one is redeemed and the many are destroyed. According to the mimetic theory the typical scenario is that the many gain a precarious peace at the cost of the one.

This difference is so important that if we remain only at the level of the biblical primal history, we must disregard an interpretation that discerns the scapegoat mechanism at work. Things are quite different, however, if we venture a reinterpretation of the mythical elements out of the total biblical context. The basis of the discovery and overcoming of the mythical world is the self-revelation of God in history. If, in the history of Israel, God reveals himself more and more clearly as that one who takes a stand for the victims of violence and lets evil fall back onto the evildoers, then the flood narrative appears as a connecting link on the way from the pre-biblical mythical narratives to the psalms of lamentation and prophetic words. In these psalms and prophetic speeches the 'floods' are expressly used as an image of human foes.[45] In demythologized form the flood narrative would indicate that the lynching of one by the many no longer completely succeeds and its sacred character falls totally apart because God saves this single victim. The consequence of this is that the many themselves go to their downfall, that is, to their self-destruction. With this new interpretation from a prophetic point of view, it appears clear that sin is more than any single event, which is what the garden and fratricide stories already suggest, as we have seen. Instead it becomes clear that after the fall the totality of human society is shaped by a structure of sinful violence. We find confirmation of this result in the narrative of the Tower of Babel where we see that the will of sinful humans to create their own self-sufficient unity is the source of deceptive projections (the tower reaching to the sky) which even more so lead to a state of confusion.

On the Historicity of the Primal History

Since the advent of critical historical studies it is usual to recognize as historical only those events for which there are sources that can withstand critical investigation. However, in the biblical primal history there are clearly mythical elements and critical witnesses for the narrated events are lacking. Therefore the judgement of secular historical research spontaneously tends to go in a negative direction. Since theology had to come to terms with the idea that in the occurrence of revelation strongly time-conditioned notions resonate, many theologians have adhered to a similar perspective. According to it one may not ascribe any historical value to the primal history, but interpret it existentially or archetypically or sociologically.[46]

Drewermann too follows this way of viewing the question, for in the third and philosophical part of his 'Structures of Evil' he asserts that everything depends on 'reading the story of Genesis 3:1–7 in such a way that it is the story of everyman insofar as it is the story of everyman's guilt before God'.[47] But with this Drewermann only poses new problems. He clearly states that evil is not necessary and so guilt exists, for it 'is not necessary that the process of anxiety leads to falling away from God and falling apart within oneself'.[48] But on the other hand he says in the same context: 'Human sin originates by necessity in the anxiety of existence' and 'the process of anxiety is necessary, and anxiety stems necessarily from freedom, indeed this is just what it is.'[49] If we take the latter statement seriously, it means that sin follows necessarily from freedom because of anxiety. Since Drewermann also makes contrary statements, one may object that we can only speak in paradox about these difficult questions. However, if paradoxical discourse is no longer distinguishable from contradictory assertions, then we can no longer distinguish it from arbitrariness. Then whether or not one wants to follow a discourse for a while depends only on the power of fascination of its images, and of the images of projected enemies, which often exert powers of fascination with devastating effects. The great tradition of patristic theology and scholasticism has therefore always taken another path and – while acknowledging the mysteriousness of God and of human freedom – it held fast to its concern for a language free of contradictions.

This concern is also important for Girard's mimetic theory, for it developed precisely out of the endeavour to interpret as consistently as possible the witness of human behaviour numerously borne by poetry, ethnology, and religion. In that it takes up a central concern of historical criticism, on the one hand, while on the other it stands in opposition to it. It passes no global judgement in the interpretation of myths. It does, to be sure, accept that in myth massive projections are at work, yet it simultaneously ventures the hypothesis that an objective historical event is concealed behind the mythical images: the collective slaying of someone who becomes a victim by chance.[50] M. Herzog therefore reproaches Girard for holding a theory that remains hypothetical and highly speculative, 'because for a historical hypothesis one should at least offer sources that have the character of empirical proof'.[51] But this demand is justified only if one accepts the traditional understanding of historical criticism as the highest norm, and yet also remains dependent on the difficulties inherent in this criticism. Girard would like to overcome the historicism in religious studies, and his method is more comparable to the historical method in the natural sciences. The theory of evolution, for example, depends on elements that come from diverse sciences with different methods. Although its work is never based on direct historical evidence, it is nevertheless able, out of the inner coherence of the theory, to report on real events and time periods in the early history of the earth and the cosmos. It is not of course able to do this in detail, but it certainly gives a broad picture. Similarly the mimetic theory sketches a scenario out of the inner coherence that it produces by the interpretation of many particular phenomena. This scenario can admittedly not be fixed at a particular point in time. Nonetheless, it wants to unearth a fundamental course of events in the beginning of a culture, indeed in the beginning of mankind as such.

If we approach the biblical story of origins with these presuppositions,[52] then we can readily accept mythical and archetypal elements in it and yet ascribe a historical nucleus to it. From this point of view, the details of how the events occurred remain, of course, hidden. This is not surprising, because the question of origins is certainly a special one in every discipline.[53] Nor does the mimetic interpretation oblige us to suppose that all evil was set in motion by one or two human beings who themselves had scarcely emerged from the animal realm. It is more likely – and this is what the primal history recounts – that evil increased among numerous people, different cultures, and through long periods of time.[54] However, since the mimetic theory accepts real events in its interpretation of myths, it holds that the same approach is appropriate in interpreting the biblical primal history. So all theological arguments whose point of departure is the original goodness of creation and which plead the cause of a fall as historical occurrence can once more obtain their full importance.[55] This means that describing guilt must no longer take refuge in paradoxical language.

Of course there are also mythical and archetypal elements in the primal history, notwithstanding the kernel of real events. For this reason we must ask whether the analysis of imitation, rivalry, and violence, as we have found it in Genesis 3–11, is the final word on the history of sin, or whether the mythical images may not conceal something deeper. This can be answered only if one starts out from that point where the Christian faith accepts a human being completely without sin who does not fall under the spell of any projections: Jesus of Nazareth.

The Synoptic Gospels report that Jesus underwent a temptation similar to what the primal history recounts concerning the first humans. Also the Tempter, in his first two attacks as presented by Matthew, seizes upon exactly the words ('If you are God's son ... ,' Matt. 4:3–6) that Jesus has just heard from his heavenly Father at the baptism ('This is my beloved son ...,' Matt. 3:17). Not only this, but he connects them directly or indirectly with the Scriptures. In doing this the Tempter offers nothing of his own but only imitates God's words. In the third attack he puts himself in a God-like position and challenges Jesus to a tribute due to God alone: to worship him, the devil. The Tempter here no longer imitates the words of God but God himself. It becomes ever more clear that the tempting voice is nothing but a covetous and perverse imitation of God.

We have precisely the same occurrence of temptation before us as in the garden story. First of all the Tempter imitates God's words in the same counterfeit way and then he himself presents a perverse image of God to be directly imitated. In one case the creator God is presented as a rival, in the other he himself as the god of this world. The great difference from the garden story is that in all three temptations Jesus, in resisting the Tempter, does not in any way let himself be drawn into the deceptive world of the enemy. He repeats only words from Scripture without adding anything to them.

Drewermann's interpretation of the primal history emphasizes Eve's act of adding to the prohibition. The mimetic analysis[56] gives special attention to that as well, but interprets it primarily as an act occurring because of the powerful pull of imitation rather than because of repressed anxiety. Since the Gospels describe the temptation of Jesus similarly to the garden story and since they speak of real events in his life, we receive an additional indication from this vantage point that the biblical narrative of origins recounts not only something archetypical, but wishes to address a real transition in the history of humanity from the situation before the fall into the human condition when the fall into sin occurred.

Imitation, Procreation, and Sin

In our analyses to this point, the mimetic, social, and historical dimension of sin has clearly appeared [*peccatum originale originans*]. However, its strange connection with the order of creation, especially as it is expressed metaphorically in the flood story, and its continuing effect from generation to generation [*peccatum originale originatum*], still remain in the dark. I propose now to cast some light also on these aspects of the question by means of another empirical theory, which in this instance stems from medical practice and was developed by A. Tomatis.[57] In Tomatis' view imitation also plays a significant role,[58] but his theory is centered primarily on hearing, language, and communication. From an evolutionary perspective he interprets the development of the simplest life forms up to human life as an intensification of the event of communication in which everything moves toward hearing. In the animal realm a development toward the ear is present already very early, and with humans hearing and speaking become the integrating factor in their manifold activities. Thus Tomatis maintains that in speaking it is not simply a matter of correctly transmitting content, but a communicating by means of the whole psyche and the entire body. Tomatis distinguishes accordingly between hearing and listening. The one who hears can understand words, true, but in contrast to the one who listens he does not resonate in his body and psyche, blocks many elements in the communication event, and therefore also receives less energy. There we come upon another key point in Tomatis' theory. He distinguishes two forms of energy: 'On the one hand, a primary nourishment insures the maintenance of the neuro-vegetative system that functions basically at the metabolic level. On the other hand, a second form of nourishment maintains the dynamics of the body and of thinking, which usually work together.'[59] The second form of energy, which is of greatest significance for mental life, is appropriated primarily through the ear. Only as a listener does the human being awaken fully to mental life.

This process already begins before birth, for Tomatis argues that the child is already a listening creature in its mother's womb. When he proposed this idea for the first time about forty years ago, his medical colleagues didn't take him seriously. In the last twenty-five years, however, numerous studies from different sides have appeared which all attest that the inner ear of the fetus is fully able to function around four and a half months and the growing child even actually reacts to the voice of its mother (its sound). This establishes the fact that the child in the womb, already before the formation of its brain, can receive and respond to real human experiences. According to Tomatis, what occurs is storage of these experiences or formation of engrams[60] in the peripheral centres of the nervous system; these experiences or engrams can, as the child matures, be elevated up to the higher levels of the brain and consciousness. He presumes that such encodings are possible already from the second month, thus already before the formation of the ear.[61] On the basis of rich experimental knowledge Tomatis even goes a step farther and ventures the hypothesis that the cell has a kind of 'memory' and that the deepest memory-traces reach back to conception.[62] Daring hypotheses like this obviously require further investigation and clarification. But precisely that which has already been ascertained shows that interhuman influences do not begin only after the fixed biological constituting of a human being. Psychological influences are already there much earlier and can have an impact on the further development and growth of the organism and the psyche. The fetus in its entirety is like an ear, the environing womb of the mother is like a speaking mouth, and the communication between the two flows into what makes the human being.

Tomatis himself sets up a metaphorical connection between his empirical theory and the garden story. Already with the title of one of his books he suggests that he understands the life of the embryo and fetus in the womb as 'nine months in paradise'.[63] He deals expressly with the symbols of the tree and the serpent and interprets both in connection with life and with hearing occurring in the mother's womb.[64] Here, he says, is where all of us feel – as in paradise – completely secure and protected and may have the experience of blissful communication. But it is in this paradise that the first strong disturbances and breaches commence. These are transmitted both through elements in the voice of the mother that betray irritation, aggression, or even hate, and through all the tensions that settle on the skin of the embryo or even on the cell wall of the first cells.

This theory obviously does not explain the actual content of the garden story as we sought to analyse it above. However, Tomatis' perspective can, to begin with, make sense of the fact that images of paradise have the capacity to waken rich associations across all cultures. These metaphorical associations also confer a certain justification on Drewermann's concerns. Beyond these associations, the knowledge of the child's hearing in the mother's womb helps us further to heed biblical data whose significance one might otherwise easily overlook. In the Book of Wisdom the speaker says about himself, 'In my mother's womb I was moulded into flesh in ten months, body and blood, from the seed of a man and the pleasure that accompanies marriage' (Wisdom 7:1–2). The psalmist goes a step farther in confessing, 'Upon you I was thrust from the womb, since birth you are my God' (Psalms 22:11; cf. Sirach 50:22). The psalmist does not just state that his entire existence is dependent upon God. Since in his confession he utilizes the metaphor of the mother's body and metaphors are not accidental, the subterranean memory of an experience of God before birth may resonate in him. A yet clearer affirmation is found in the songs of the Servant of the Lord, where the deep insight into the vicarious suffering of evil also appears. The Servant says of himself, 'The Lord called me from birth, from my mother's womb he gave me my name' (Isaiah 49:1). An abstract theology sees in this affirmation a mere metaphor for the idea that the Servant knows with certainty he has been called. By contrast, Tomatis alerts us that recollecting our earliest experiences belongs to our total experience. So the interpretation that suggests itself from Tomatis' research is that the experience of being called was so intensive, it simultaneously awakened in the prophet memory traces that reached back into his life in his mother's womb. Something similar seems also to hold for Paul, for he says that God set him apart from his mother's womb (Galatians 1:15). We find the most explicit indication, however, in the narrative of John the Baptist. In the announcement of his birth the angel foretells that he is filled with the Holy Spirit already in his mother's womb (Luke 1:15), and the Gospel reports later how the child reacts and leaps as soon as it hears the voice of Mary (Luke 1:41, 44). Narratives like these don't merely deal with vague metaphors, but address experiences we should particularly consider apart from the historical critical value of individual accounts.

The Bible also reports positive as well as negative experiences that already begin in the mother's womb. Jeremiah curses the day of his birth (Jeremiah 20:14), and Job laments that he did not die in his mother's womb (Job 10:18). The psalmist speaks especially clearly when he says, 'Against you alone I have sinned, I have done what is evil in your sight ... Truly I was born in guilt, in iniquity I was conceived' (Psalms 51:6–7). Traditional theology has relied on this psalm passage in teaching that original sin is propagated through sexual intercourse. But the context in the psalm doesn't fit that doctrine. The psalmist confesses above all his own sin and moves from there back to the sin of his mother when she conceived him. Thus he may indicate an event of communication – or better, a disturbance of communication – which from the beginning burdened the relations between him, his God, and his mother. Job seems to think in a similar vein when he says,

> Man born of woman is few of days
> and full of trouble.
> Like a flower that springs up and fades,
> swift as a shadow that does not remain.
> O that clean could come from unclean,
> but there is none. (Job 14:1–2, 4)

If a clean person cannot come from an unclean one, then it is not simply a matter of negative influence in later years. Humans who are 'born of woman' are so deeply bound to one another through reproduction and birth that uncleanness too is passed on through the communication that is disturbed from the very beginning.

From the perspective gained let us once more turn back to the biblical primal history because procreation plays also an important role in it. Previously we did not go into the genealogical lists (Genesis 4:17–22; 5:1–32; 10:1–32). The recurrence of 'begetting', which is otherwise almost stereotypical, is rewritten in a more detailed way at the beginning of the 'record of the descendants of Adam' (Gen. 5:1). The text begins with a repetition of the statement in Gen. 1:26 that man was created 'in the likeness of God' and blessed. The text continues, 'Adam was one hundred and thirty years old when he begot a son in his likeness, after his image, and he named him Seth' (Gen. 5:3). Here begetting a descendant is directly linked to the creative activity of God, and this connection is brought to bear on the concept of likeness and image. As God created human beings in his image (Gen. 1:26), so God grants Adam [mankind] the begetting of descendants in his image. The text thus emphasizes how closely humans are bound to one another through procreation. Adam does not simply produce a new body, as for example the body that God formed 'from the clay of the ground' (Gen. 2:7) and had then to breathe the breath of life into it. On the contrary, he and his wife are granted to produce a living creature in full similarity to them. This metaphorical language suggests that procreation is much more than a biological occurrence. It must be understood more in Tomatis' sense as a communicative image-formation in which the parents and the fruit of their bodies work together in the closest way.

Let us take note of a further aspect. In the primal history there are two genealogies that stem from Adam, the one line from Cain to Lamech and the other from Seth to Noah. Therefore it is often said that the narrator intended to set the latter line of descent in direct opposition to the former one.[65] Differences between them are certainly indisputable, for the line of Cain leads to Lamech, who sought revenge seventy-sevenfold, while Noah comes out of the line of Seth, and through him humanity is rescued. But this distinction should not be made hard and fast because in the line of Seth too there are only two men who appear before God as righteous, namely Enoch and Noah (Gen. 5:24; 6:9).

In stressing the contrast between the genealogies interpreters have often referred to what Eve says when Seth is born: 'God has granted me another son instead of Abel, because Cain killed him' (Gen. 4:25).[66] However, there are weighty reasons against the interpretation of these words as a direct contrast to the genealogy of Cain: Firstly, the line of Seth is reckoned in the 'record of the descendants of Adam' (Gen. 5:1–32), and Eve's words (Gen. 4:25) don't belong to this list, for it begins in Genesis 5:1 once again expressly with the creation. Secondly, the genealogy always proceeds from the firstborn son, who begets another firstborn. Thus in Gen. 5:3 Adam also names his son Seth, and likewise in 4:26 Seth names his firstborn Enosh. In 4:25, though, it is Eve who speaks and she sets Seth not in opposition to the line of Cain, but she states that God granted her as a substitute for her slain son Abel. So in 4:25 it is not a man who establishes a genealogy, but Eve, the wife and mother, expresses the consolation that she was granted a replacement for the loss of Abel through the birth of another son.

Consequently, procreation and childbearing have an eminently positive significance in the biblical primal history, in two regards. On the one hand, humans participate in this way directly in the creative power of God, which is part of the original goodness of creation (Gen. 1:27f.; 2:21–24; 5:1–3). By this means, on the other hand, a replacement is provided for all those who constantly fall victim to violence and death (Gen. 4:25f.). The primal history views procreation and childbearing as the great counter-forces to the destructive power of sin and violence, creative counter-forces that make life possible after the fall and offer ever new comfort and hope. But in spite of its eminent positive significance sin penetrates also into this sphere of life, for it interrupts the harmony of the sexes (Gen. 3:7, 16), and the woman must bear children in pain (Gen. 3:16). Indeed, it is just in this sphere of creativity that complete perversion can come about. The 'record of the descendants of Adam' (Gen. 5:1), which with every family head formulaically repeats after the birth of the firstborn son : 'and begot sons and daughters' (5:4, 7, 10, 13, 16, 19, 22, 26, 30), is immediately followed by the narrative of the sons of God. The latter begins: 'When people began to multiply on earth and daughters were born to them, the sons of God[67] saw how beautiful the daughters of men were, so they took for their wives as many of them as they chose' (Gen. 6:1f.). Here the seemingly good line of Seth, from which many people come, leads directly to perversion of a sexual kind. The creaturely participation in the creative power of God in procreation becomes in 'overstepping of bounds'[68] a deed in which divine and human mingle in a way that contradicts the order of creation.[69] The invasion of sin into the power of creativity has consequences immediately in this dimension of human life: the Lord shortens the human life span (Gen. 6:3). Because humans are so profoundly bound to one another through procreation and because sin has struck this sphere also with its curse, evil spreads further over this life force, which in itself is positive. The complex narrative of Genesis 5–6 again takes up the creation of mankind, then relates how Adam begets his son, continues with the genealogy, and forms a transition to the misdeed of the sons of God, in order finally to arrive at the statement that the earth is corrupt and filled with violence in God's eyes. These narrative links leading to God's judgement of the earth's corruption must therefore not be accidental. By means of this great narrative arc the text succeeds in describing how sin corrupted even positive creative forces and attained universal dominion through its penetration into the creative power of humankind.

So we have come up with two important questions for systematic interpretation of the primal history:

1. Does the spread of sin via imitation, as we have previously elaborated, have something to do with its propagation through sexual intercourse?
2. How can sin take possession of a power that belongs completely to the goodness of the created order?

For both questions the biblical passages about being called in the mother's womb and being conceived in sin suggest an answer, if they are opened up by means of Tomatis' theory to the full extent of their systematic importance. The event encompassed by 'begetting' and 'conceiving' is accordingly much more than a mere biological occurrence: it is a communicative process that includes the whole human person, an especially intensive imaging ('in his image') and imitating that extends into the human body in the most profound way. Yet it doesn't remain bodily or fleshly, but has effect in the whole being. Because interhuman communication is disrupted through sin and procreation belongs to this communication, sin can make its home in the deepest dimension of human nature.

Synopsis

The question of original sin is complex and includes different areas of research. By way of review three levels are to be distinguished: that of natural history, of the human history of freedom, and of supernatural calling.[70] At the same time though we should see these levels in their interconnection, for in actual human beings they penetrate one another mutually.

Natural History

Natural history is nowadays interpreted through the theory of evolution, which also deals with the origin of mankind,[71] For a theology of original sin it is not merely the question of origins that is meaningful. Since the theory of evolution outlines a universal conceptual framework that fundamentally influences contemporary thought, it also easily predisposes judgements in other spheres. Thus we must very briefly look at elements in this theory that are subliminally important as a conceptual model for original sin [as past event that now affects everyone].

According to more recent research, all higher atoms on the earth that are necessary for life are such that they could not have originated in our solar system. They must have been formed in a gigantic earlier solar system and then become 'dust' through a violent explosion out of which our solar system was able to emerge.[72] Our body is therefore not simply a product of our earth, but in it we preserve traces of primeval events in the cosmos and we are able to live thanks only to these traces. Something analogous seems to hold concerning the genetic code, which amazingly is the same for all life forms on the earth. We can best explain this uniformity – along with the likewise similar right-left asymmetry in all biological processes – by assuming that all living cells stem from a single primordial cell.[73] Both cases, which can be multiplied by additional examples, thus lead to a conceptual model according to which a concrete event happening long ago continues to have such an effect that within certain limits it is determinative of everything to come. A conceptual model like this shows that today, in contrast to the Enlightenment, we cannot assume a fundamental opposition between particular historical events and general truths. If we can explain general structures out of particular events in nature, then we also must be more cautious in this regard about human history, which remains bound to natural history.

A further suggestion taken from the doctrine of evolution is worthy of note for our question about imitation. All information in a living cell is stored in the great DNA molecule, and the ability of this molecule to create exact copies of itself belongs to the basic character of living processes.[74] Cells can multiply, divide, and produce identical offshoot cells. This occurrence of replication is a prerequisite for the development of sexuality, which plays a huge role in evolution and leads to the origin of species.[75] Even the ability to imitate is developed finally out of the fundamental ability of copying, after many intermediate steps. The ability to imitate shapes the life of the highest animals, above all that of the apes, and is 'the unconditional prerequisite for the beginning of language'.[76] Through this new capability of imitation it is possible to pass on earlier events not simply by the genetic code, but directly and pointedly from one member of the species to the other and from one generation to the other. Also, from this point of view some correlations between sexuality and imitation can be seen. We can note the correlation in the mating behaviour of many animals, in which imitation plays a large role. The meaning of procreation seen in light of a comprehensively understood process of communication and imitation, as the work of Tomatis has produced for us, may thus be understood as a fitting part of a long evolutionary pre-history.

The History of Nature and of Human Freedom

According to church doctrine as officially formulated at the Council of Trent, original sin is passed on through reproduction [*propagatione*] and not through imitation [*imitatione*].[77] This use of language suggests a stark contrast between two spheres of which one, reproduction, seems to be purely natural, while in the other, that of imitation, freedom also plays a role. But our analyses until now suggest the idea that this antithesis is rather problematic. In the mimetic theory imitation is described as both natural – as a kind of quasi-osmotic contact – and also historical, as free choice between true mimesis and covetous imitation. It does not begin first with the already constituted subject but plays a decisive role in the development of the ego. Tomatis' theory elaborates the communicative and mimetic processes in the development of the subject yet more precisely. For one thing it illuminates the unity of the bodily and spiritual components in linguistic communication, and for another it posits this process as beginning in the mother's womb, indeed already in the process of procreation. Since the human being in this earliest phase of development is uniquely open to the influences of environment,[78] it is sensible to conclude that disturbances at the beginning of its development have an especially profound effect. Aggressive elements in the initial process of communication take effect on its further growth and may even enter into the physical and psychic structure of its organism. Evil migrates thus from generation to generation, and so it is understandable that people may speak of 'hereditary transmission'. This comprehensively understood 'hereditary transmission' no longer stands in opposition to imitation. Rather it designates a differentiated basic process that can be only be adequately described by utilizing complementary concepts stemming from different paradigms.

With a new meaning of 'hereditary transmission' we have not yet completely reached the decisive point in the doctrine of original sin. If humankind already has a negative imprint in its development, then it seems to be more the victim of evil than being sinful itself. This question can be clarified to an extent along the lines of what we have already worked out. The theories of Girard and Tomatis proceed, to be sure, from empirical knowledge [quite different in each case]. However, since they describe human beings in their total behaviour, they advance to a basic desire that from the very beginning drives beyond all individual needs and is of an unbounded, metaphysical kind.[79]

Unbounded desire always has, however, a moral character. Further, Girard and Tomatis accept that this boundless desire has already, prior to its own free decision, been formed, whether through quasi-osmotic contact with an alien desire (Girard) or through an awakening call in the mother's womb (Tomatis). Since human beings now live in a world of violence and death and are imprinted with a deep existential anxiety, at least for the situation after the fall, as Drewermann rightly perceives, they have accordingly a mutual effect on one another. They awaken in one another not only trust and love, but they induce others through open or concealed aggressiveness to defend themselves and to become inwardly enclosed in their own deep desiring. The trust with which the creative power of procreation was endowed is instinctively permeated by a deep mistrust, so in the resulting fruit of the body not only love and the will to life, but also at the same time anxiety and egotism, will be awakened. So it is that this fundamental desire turns away from its true goal. Thus humans are indeed born as victims of their preceding aggressive and violent humanity. Their own unbounded desiring belongs to the sphere of morality but becomes diverted from its goal, from God. Therefore they inherently have – prior to their own decision – a 'sinful' character. Due to this entanglement of fundamental desiring with others, adult humans cannot really be converted through their own personal act of freedom: only by passing over into a new community, which encompasses all their desiring, is a true renewal possible.

Supernatural Calling in Human History

The supernatural dimension opens up in connection with the question of the meaning of the entirety of human history[80] and a centre of history is needed in order to recognize this meaning. For the Christian faith Jesus as the Christ is this centre, which comprises the beginning and the end,[81] so the supernatural dimension of sin can only be known if we start from him. Thus even though the biblical primal history already precisely presents the dynamics of sin, a proper doctrine of original sin is found first in the New Testament. The theological tradition has certainly accepted that before the fall Adam had a full and extraordinary knowledge of God's saving ways because his knowledge was untroubled. This view, however, misunderstands the peculiar character of supernatural history; it separates it from natural history and the history of freedom and makes of it a superstructure.[82] The history of revelation gives witness that the supernatural dimension plays itself out completely in the human history of freedom and in natural history. Biblical narrative also shows that the full extent of sin does not suddenly burst in, but increases over many generations. Even if sin, seen from the standpoint of God, always has its same radical character, yet from the human standpoint it immediately appears in a history in which many reciprocally connected members work together.[83]

The radical character of sin therefore remains hidden from the awareness of every individual for the most part. As humans never fully grasp their deepest desiring and are never fully in control of it, so also the knowledge of supernatural history, sin and responsibility for sin is always partially removed from them. For this reason it is in principle impossible to determine more precisely the degree of clarity and the extent of responsibility that those people had with whom the history of sin actually began. It is theoretically conceivable that the first sin carrying full theological significance could have begun with scarcely a notice on the empirical level and occurred in a form of consciousness whose explicit contents still stood very close to that of the animals. One can therefore 'interpret the meaning of sin as mankind's sinful continuation in a naturalness, which becomes precisely unnatural in that it does not transcend itself according to its own endowment'.[84] These ideas are possibly correct. However, we know neither the concrete circumstances nor the degree of clarity nor the extent of responsibility, as just stated. So with full acceptance of a real history of sin we can make no concrete individual responsible, no Adam and no Eve, for all human evil. If we do it anyway, we are only creating scapegoats.

On the Question of Theodicy

If we are not able clearly to attribute the responsibility for evil, then the tendency emerges almost instinctively to push the question further: why did God create a world in which such great evils appear almost spontaneously, indeed almost as a matter of course? This question cannot be treated here in detail, and furthermore it can be answered only within certain limits. Because we have basically defended the historicity of the primal history, it follows that the traditional answer explaining moral evil on the basis of human freedom is fundamentally correct. What we have worked out in this study indicates why God takes on the risk of creaturely freedom.

When God created the human being 'from the soil of the earth' (Gen. 2:7) on the one hand, and as similar to him and in his image (Gen. 1:26) on the other hand, then this being is necessarily caught in an extreme tension. As creatures created from nothing, human beings are also called to participation in the divine life. Therefore they are not complete within themselves, but take part in three histories – which is to say that they are extremely decentered. Because we are completely in the image of others, in the image of God and our parents, our action is instinctively directed toward others – toward God and fellow humans. We are sustained and moved by imitation, which functions in a quasi-osmotic way. Since we cannot immediately know or experience our true model, God, we necessarily fall very easily into the power of a deceptive model. The step from the imitation of God to imitation of an idol can come to pass almost imperceptibly. This is not to raise a question about God's goodness, but it certainly shows that the infinite God cannot impart his glory to a very limited creature without exposing it to extreme stress and thus to great danger. God is no rival to human beings and he would grant them everything he has of unending good; just for this reason he must require of them the risk of encounter with him, although this exceeds their proper human powers.

Notes

1 Wiedenhofer, 'Zum gegenwärtigen Stand der Erbsündentheologie'.
2 Ibid., 366.
3 Drewermann, *Strukturen des Bösen*.
4 Ricoeur, *Symbolik des Bösen*. Cf. Also Pottier, 'Interpréter le péché original sur les traces de G. Fessard', 809–810.
5 Wiedenhofer, 'Erbsündentheologie', 355.
6 Drewermann, *Strukturen des Bösen* I, 59.
7 Ibid., 59–60.
8 'However, anxiety is an ambiguous word. Psychologically it takes guilt from an event and causes everything to appear to be compulsory' (ibid., 78).
9 Ibid., 95.
10 Ibid., 146.
11 'In the division of the primal history it is clear that God intervenes only indirectly after Cain's murder of his brother, and after the great flood he certainly no longer intervenes immediately in the affairs of mankind; rather, he allows them to continue until the final social catastrophe' (ibid., 319).
12 'The attitude of Lamech in the primal history lays the foundation for the horror of history; and the augmentation of cultural, technical, and political progress must proceed along with a rise in the frightfulness of reciprocal murder as long as the spirit of Lamech remains the basis of history. This dead-end, in which the increase in the curve of technical accomplishment must proceed by way of a simultaneous increase of alienation from God, is remarkable' (ibid., 156).
13 Ibid., 177f.
14 Ibid., 206. 'The order of nature continues not simply due to God's

creative work but through his compassionate resolve to protect nature from human corruption and the destruction of both in their turn by human corruption' (ibid., 228).

15 Ibid., 247.

16 Ibid., 313; 314. 'It is precisely this character of necessity in the case of a given sin that is so unnerving' (319).

17 Ibid., 315.

18 Drewermann, *Strukturen des Bösen*, 2, 616.

19 It agrees at important points with G. von Rad, *Old Testament Theology*, I, 154–160. On the other hand, he disagrees with C. Westermann, who holds that all the primal history narratives are of equal status and intend only to show different possibilities for committing sin. On the arguments of Westermann, cf. Oberforcher, *Die Flutprologe*, 333–348.

20 Ibid., 617.

21 'This mode of imitation operates with a quasi-osmotic immediacy necessarily betrayed and lost in all the dualities of the modern problematic of desire, including the conscious and unconscious.' Girard, *To Double Business Bound*, 89.

22 On the whole historical-religious background and its transformation cf. Baudler, *Erlösung vom Stiergott*.

23 Girard, *Job, the Victim of His People*, 154–168.

24 On these themes cf. Schwager, *Must There Be Scapegoats?*, 91–109.

25 Cf. Hamerton-Kelly, *Sacred Violence*, 91.

26 Cf. Judges 2:12, 19; 1 Kings 14:24; 18:18; 2 Kings 17:15, 19; 2 Chronicles 36:14; Jeremiah 2:8, 23, 25; 7:6, 9; 8:2; 9:13; 11:10; 13:10; 16:11; 25:6; 35:15.

27 'The intrinsic connection with the adamah – once the opening to the basic movement toward life – becomes the expression of the exclusive tendency toward death.' Oberforcher, *Flutprologe*, 242.

28 Cf. Ibid., 236–243.

29 Further reasons supporting the close connection are given in N. Lohfink, 'Wie sollten man das Alte Testament auf die Erbsünde hin befragen?' In *Zum Problem der Erbsünde*, 9–52; for the reference here, 37–41. Cf. Also Girard, *Shakespeare. Les feux de l'envie*, 396.

30 The narrative of fratricide introduces a new element: rivalry has its origin in connection with sacrifice. In view of the great significance that ritual sacrifice had in the history of religions and also in Israel, this circumstance cannot be unimportant. However, biblical exegesis has scarcely found a satisfying explanation for it. It appears to me that N. Lohfink has gone the furthest in explaining it: 'The sacrifice of Abel accomplished its intention but Cain's did not. This is how we must interpret the assertion that Yahweh had regard for Abel and his offering but not for Cain and his offering. But how does it look to human eyes if a sacrifice does not accomplish its intention, if an intended result does not occur? The answer is now narrated in the story. Cain is overcome with rage, his face falls – just like the steer that breaks and runs away. The brothers' latent jealousy and rivalry are already plainly indicated by the fact that they both, side by side and at the same time, do the same thing.

Evidently the act of sacrifice is intended to suppress and soften their jealousy and rivalry. This is the result in Abel's case, while Cain's offering fails and so evil first fully breaks out. If this interpretation is right, then the narrative presupposes a concept of the social meaning of their sacrifices which is in accord with Girard's theory.' Lohfink, 'Wie sollte man das Alte Testament auf die Erbsünde hin befragen?', 43–44.

31 Since the sin lying in wait is described as like a demon, J. Williams sees quite correctly a connection between the serpent and sin. Williams, *The Bible, Violence, and the Sacred*, 35.

32 We can also confirm this conclusion from our study of the whole Old Testament, for it characteristically presents the judgement of God as violent destruction by a hostile human hand. Cf. Schwager, *Must There Be Scapegoats?*, 53–70.

33 Cf. Gen. 14:1–24; Ju. 8:22–29, 30; 1 Sam. 8:1–22; Isa. 14:13f.; Jer. 51:53f.

34 Paul presents the relation between sin and law in a similar vein (Rom. 7:7–13).

35 Cf. Hamerton-Kelly, *Sacred Violence*, 92–97.

36 Williams, *The Bible, Violence, and the Sacred*, 35.

37 Myths are a product of this concealment according to the mimetic theory. This view is fully compatible with the fact that the biblical primal history both reaches back to myths and simultaneously transforms them profoundly. In doing this it at least partially uncovers the human forces that are hidden behind the mythical gods.

38 Cf. Girard, *Things Hidden Since the Foundation of the World*, 144–149.

39 Cf. Schwager, *Must There Be Scapegoats?*, 53–71, 109–135.

40 Oberforcher, *Flutprologe*, 354.

41 Ibid., 399–510.

42 Ibid., 412.

43 Ibid., 479; cf. 424–433, 647. Within the history of Israel's faith this expansion should be clarified by reference to the Priestly source's response to exile. After the Babylonian Exile the Priestly narrative transposed the corruption 'from a preeminently prophetic to a primal historical context, or from a political and social to a general context of humans and creation' (ibid., 479).

44 Whereas God gave all animals only the 'green plants for food' (Gen. 1:31) in the beginning, killing in the animal world is even regarded as normal after the flood, for 'fear and dread' shall now come upon all animals (Gen. (9:2). In the future requital will be made only for killing of humans by other humans or by animals.

45 Cf. Ps. 32:6; 69:16; 88:18; 93:6; Isa. 8:7f.; 17:12; 28:15, 18; Jer. 47:2; Ezek. 27:34.

46 Cf. Baumann, *Erbsünde?*; Duffy, *Our Hearts of Darkness*.

47 Drewermann, *Strukturen des Bösen* III, 427.

48 Ibid., 545.

49 Ibid.

50 To justify this hypothesis Girard refers, inter alia, to medieval persecution texts in which historical criticism accepts precisely the

same conclusion, namely that real events are mixed with projections. Cf. Girard, *The Scapegoat*, 1–56.

51 Herzog, *Religionstheorie und Theologie René Girards*, 133.

52 On the scientific character of a comprehensive theory, especially with regard to theology, cf. Kreiner, *Ende der Wahrheit?*, 475–576.

53 Cf. *Understanding Origins*.

54 In this respect quite different scenarios are theoretically conceivable. Humanity could have split off into different branches that fell into cul-de-sacs and died out (e.g., the Neanderthals). In great crises they may also have propagated themselves in a very narrow way, perhaps even through an individual woman. All that remains open to paleontological research.

55 Cf. Rahner, *Grundkurs des Glaubens*, 116–120. This in no way means that before the condition of historical guilt anything concrete is accessible to us; starting from our condition – in guilt – we can only get back to the beginning of this condition, but we have no vantage point allowing us to unlock the concrete state of things before that.

56 For further verification of analysis of rivalry and violence within the New Testament, cf. Schwager, *Jesus in the Drama of Salvation*, 29–118.

57 For a complete exposition of this theory, cf. Schwager, *Hörer des Wortes*.

58 Cf. Tomatis, *L'oreille et la vie*, 80f, 140f.; idem., *L'oreille et la voix*, 21.

59 Tomatis, *Der Klang des Lebens*, 100f.

60 On the biological and neurological basis for engrams, cf. Bresch, *Zwischenstufe Leben*, 177–188.

61 Tomatis, *L'oreille et la vie*, 329. 'From anatomical and physiological investigations I knew that at four and a half months the fetus was in a position to react to sounds. Its ear is ordinarily formed by this age. The development of the inner ear and hearing ossicles [in the middle ear] is anatomically completed. The system of the inner ear has reached its final size. The hearing nerve, the first to be myelinated [have nerve cells matured], takes up its function and so enters into its active phase when the embryo begins to move and becomes a fetus, after four and a half months of intrauterine life. Yet in my conception the apparatus of the cavity [vestibule] leading into the cochlea works much earlier already. Even if perception is still not integrated into consciousness – in direct form as we commonly understand it – yet there is already a reaction. The reaction shows that what happens is an activation of the metameric reflex arcs under vestibular control. Also at earlier points in time the stimulus of sound may very well bring forth reactions, ones, to be sure, that are essentially confined to the skin.' Tomatis, *Klang des Lebens*, 61f.

62 'Under the effect of a treatment basically of filtered sounds [electronic ear], the subjects revealed images of their cellular life: images of descent into the uterine tube, fixation on the uterus … The drawings demonstrate that there is memory from the moment there is a cell. The cell and the memory work hand in hand.' Tomatis, *Neuf*

mois au Paradis, 173; cf. 17, 120, 180, 191.

63 Tomatis, *Neuf mois au Paradis*.

64 Ibid., 129–131. He says, ' ... like the snake who remains deaf outside the water, aware only of some vibrations ... The snake has a brain already well developed ... but he is deaf as a jug! I always say that he's the one who taught humans not to listen' (ibid., 88f.).

65 For the discussion of this question, cf. Oberforcher, *Flutprologe*, 284–309.

66 Cf. Ibid., 300f.

67 The Hebrew could be translated either 'sons of God' or 'sons of the gods'. 'Divine beings' is a possible translation. (Tr.).

68 Oberforcher, *Flutprologe*, 316.

69 The biblical narrative may have originated in myths of 'sacred marriage' and the practice of sacral prostitution bound up with that. These myths were particularly widespread in the ancient Near East. Cf. Heiler, *Die Frau in den Religionen der Menschheit*, 27–29; Herodotus, *History* I/II.

70 G. Fessard has elaborated the distinction among these three levels especially clearly and reflectively. Fessard, *L'Histoire et ses trois niveaux d'historicité*.

71 On the questions that the evolutionary approach produces, G. Martelet in particular has gone thoroughly into original sin in his book, *Libre réponse à un scandale*.

72 'Also all matter of our planet, which almost all is composed of higher atom nuclei, has its origin thus in stars that exploded more than five billion years ago. That means also that – apart from hydrogen – all atoms from which our human bodies are composed were formed billions of years ago through nuclear processes in some gigantic star or the other. They then participated in such tremendous primordial events – somewhere – at some time – in the early period of our galaxy.' Bresch, *Zwischenstufe Leben*, 46.

73 Cf. ibid., 116.

74 Cf. Ibid., 81–90.

75 Ibid., 125–130.

76 Ibid., 193.

77 DH 1513.

78 Note also the imprint phases of animals.

79 Girard speaks explicitly of a 'metaphysical desire' (*Deceit, Desire, and the Novel*, 83–85, 256–314), and Tomatis speaks of listening to the cosmos and the divine logos (*Klang des Lebens*, 169–182;' Ecouter, c'est se convertir').

80 C.f. Fessard, *L'Histoire et ses trois niveaux d'historicité*, 349.

81 Ibid., 354.

82 'Indeed, this history that bestows meaning does not itself appear except upon a foundation of human and natural history' (ibid., 350).

83 To be sure, Paul states clearly that sin came into the world through *one* man, but he emphasizes just as much that death came to all because *all* have sinned (Rom. 5:12). Consequently his formulation permits no precise determination of guilt. For Paul it's not a matter

of a precise attribution of guilt; this is shown by the fact that he completely passes over Eve, who is the first person to sin according to the biblical narrative.

84 Spaemann, 'Über einige Schwierigkeiten', in Schönborn, *Zur kirchlichen Erbsündelehre*, 65.

Chapter 2

Evolution, Sin, and Genetic Technology

Our understanding of redemption is very closely connected to how we construe sin and original sin. H.U. von Balthasar was able to show that Maximus Confessor developed his teaching of salvation in Christ 'with almost geometrical strictness', in accord with his 'anthropology of original sin'.[1] What may be said about Maximus holds more or less for all great authors who have made an important contribution to the doctrine of redemption.[2] But one could also say the reverse. A doctrine of original sin can be finally clarified only on the basis of an understanding of redemption.

Agreeing with this traditional view, I have previously sought to deepen the doctrines of sin,[3] original sin,[4] and redemption through a multifaceted inquiry and to expand these to a dramatic model.[5] In these works the question of evolution was addressed only incidentally. Therefore I propose to go into this subject more fully[6] and deal with the primary question it poses: whether and how the new forms of knowledge about the evolutionary development of humankind may be integrated into a more profound doctrine of original sin and into a dramatic doctrine of redemption. There are no clear precedents, either from Scripture or from the tradition or contemporary theology, so I can here venture only a hypothesis whose persuasiveness has to be demonstrated in future discussion by the light it sheds on other topics of thought and research.

The History of Sin of 'Homo Habilis' or 'Homo Erectus'

The tradition of the Church teaches that original sin involves not only an existential dimension of present human life but also an event, an act of sin, in the beginning of mankind. From an evolutionary perspective this teaching is by no means as improbable as is often asserted. Rather, just the opposite is suggested. Certainly since Haeckel the biogenetic principle, according to which ontogeny (= development of the embryo) recapitulates phylogeny (= history of the people or race) in a reduced manner, plays a significant role. Although this principle was qualified by further research, it retained its significance; in certain respects it has even become expanded in recent decades. The organisms of creatures today are understood more and more as 'living memories', and this holds in fact both for the history of the human race and the history of the cosmos. The elementary particles out of which organisms developed may have originated, according to the currently dominant hypothesis, shortly after the primordial explosion, the 'big bang'. The elements were formed in the remote past. In this way almost all of our planet's matter, which is predominantly composed of higher atom nuclei, stems 'from stars that exploded more than five billion years ago. That means that apart from hydrogen all atoms which make up our human body were formed billions of years ago through nuclear processes in some gigantic star or the other and then participated in tremendous primordial events – somewhere – at some time in the early period of our galaxy.'[7] Also events in the early period of our earth determine us today. The genetic code, which is similar for all living creatures, suggests that all present life originated in a single primordial cell and extends the memory of its origin until today through this uniform code.[8] So at ever new levels we see that organisms living today have a 'memory' that extends back to determinative events and 'bifurcations' in the earlier history of the cosmos and of life. Humans belong to these organisms. From this viewpoint, therefore, a doctrine is not surprising which holds that all present humans bear within themselves the memory of another form of bifurcation, of a deviation from the right way in the beginning of human history. Certainly the question of freedom here raises an utterly new problem.[9] But what we consider sensible regarding this question depends in considerable part on the conception we form of all reality, and this conception today is more in favour of the doctrine of original sin than against it.

Of course, according to modern scientific knowledge humanity is far older than the Bible supposed. Paleontological research characterizes homo habilis who appeared about two million years ago, as already man.[10] Whether this creature was also a human in the philosophical sense is admittedly debatable.[11] Certainly, however, humanity as such is very old (*homo erectus*), and the brain size of the first humans was decisively smaller than now.[12] This raises the question as to what consequences the small brain size could have had for earlier human behaviour and how one should conceive sin under these circumstances.

For human beings in the philosophical sense we must assume an openness to the absolute and along with that an unlimited desire. Among the first humans this desiring may have moulded a creature that, because of its smaller brain size, was far less able to ponder its own deeds rationally than men can in the present. Admittedly the most recent investigations of the manlike apes show that the possibilities for conscious differentiating in the transition from animal to human may be more complex than we usually suppose.[13] Yet the much smaller brain capacity forces us to the conclusion that the first humans had above all a very intensive emotional life or 'life-feeling'[14] in which the relation to the infinite ground of life was embedded.[15] There are no fundamental difficulties with attributing to this early human consciousness the capacity of decision-making.[16] Characteristic of freedom is that a being forms its life out of itself,[17] and this dimension of freedom is even more fitting in an evolutionary rather than a static world. In an evolutionary world the total created reality, notwithstanding its fundamental dependence on God, develops out of itself in a certain fashion. Also characteristic of freedom is the possibility of choice. We can certainly not conceive this potential of the first humans as a clear decision between two rationally clear and comprehensible alternatives, but it should be thought of as the ability to be faithful or unfaithful to a received gift or endowment.[18] The first humans accordingly had been called to respond to the vaguely felt, gift-like experience of the closeness of God in great emotional nearness and intensity, but in a very limited capacity of self-reflection. The 'fulguration' or the emergence by which they arose out of the animal realm (speaking scientifically), or the self-transcendence by which they became human through the creative action of God (speaking theologically), would have led to opening up in them an utterly new feeling of immeasurable vastness with intensive emotional clarity. These early breakthrough experiences should have prompted them to outgrow the reactions of creatures in the animal world.[19] However, as the doctrine of original sin states, there were already negative decisions in the beginning, so we must reckon that the strong emotional character of the first humans rapidly provoked the most intense conflicts and altercations. In these conflicts and altercations the initially positive mechanisms achieved during evolution in the animal realm now became operative in a perverted form. We can therefore 'interpret the meaning of sin as mankind's sinful continuation in a naturalness, which becomes precisely unnatural in that it does not transcend itself according to its own endowment'.[20] So in this respect one should not think merely in terms of a fall that occurred at one specific time. Everything could have begun with a seemingly harmless[21] slipping away from the original gift-like experience or with a well-intended, yet forced rekindling of an earlier good feeling that soon led as fixation to new, bad habits, and this had consequences which far surpassed the harmless beginning.[22]

The Bible relates that the first act of violence (Cain-Abel) followed the first sin, and the violence expanded (Lamech) with the consequence that the earth before the great flood 'became corrupt in God's eyes and was full of violence' (Genesis 6:11). The latter passage corresponds surprisingly well to what we can imagine concerning the beginnings of humankind. Violence has certainly already increased among the highest animals. 'The brutality of chimpanzee battles is without compare in the animal world and is paralleled among humans ... In its emotional structure and brutality, in motivation, context of origination, and function their group struggles resemble human relations in a startling kind and manner.'[23] Because of their small brain size and great emotionality the altercations and conflicts among the first humans likewise may have been so great that for a long time humanity, as the biblical flood narrative indicates, was subject to an endangered existence. In contrast to the mythical language of the flood narrative the danger certainly did not threaten from the side of God, nor in the first place from nature, but primarily from other humans.[24] How, in spite of this, did mankind survive? It was due less to its reason than to its spontaneous tendency instinctively to divert the aggressive potential in a group outward against a victim or an enemy (scapegoat mechanism).[25] This polarization created coherence in human groups. Moreover, survival was made easier by the circumstance of plenty of room for the first humans to separate spatially from other humans.

Evolution within Sinful Mankind

According to our spontaneous perception, the brain growth of human beings took a very long time (perhaps almost two million years). But measured in the usual time periods of evolution, it proceeded very rapidly. Indeed, we are probably dealing here with a singular evolutionary speed. Many scholars attribute this striking phenomenon directly to human aggression and suspect (C. Bresch, for example) that reciprocal killing was an important instrument for the rapid brain development. Bresch says, 'It is difficult to refute the hypothesis that humans themselves through combat with one another and through destruction of subjugated groups were the most important instrument of their own selection, which produced a rapid further development of their brains.'[26] He clarifies the hypothesis in this way:

> If, however, a limited killing of one's own kind is once established, this then becomes a new instrument of selection, because the stronger, faster reacting, more intelligent animals survive ... The more intelligent horde had better chances of survival. Its communication was more intense, its tools, weapons, were more effective. Its foresight was more far-reaching and so its ability to exist in an unfavourable environment increased. Man himself provided for the selection of better brains.[27]

The idea that human being took an active part in its own evolution may easily be related to the Christian doctrine of creation and to Christian anthropology. According to these, human beings must become and form what they are and should be through themselves, as their freedom and responsibility for themselves show.[28] This truth is valid first of all with respect to the individual. Yet it only takes on its full importance when extended to the idea that human beings have taken an active part in their own evolution.

Bresch's hypothesis certainly needs to be supplemented to prevent misunderstanding. Mutation and selection, the classical factors of evolution, can only be effective if they are sustained by a 'will to life'. We see this 'will' in the animal world as a striving for survival, and this means specifically that the single individuals actively seek food and protect their lives actively through flight from or defence against enemies. The 'will to life' is manifested also in the striving to propagate and the care of the new generation. The role of sexuality in evolution is now ever more strongly emphasized in research.[29] So it is that we now see in a new light the significance the uniting of organisms had within evolution. Great evolutionary steps became possible when different organisms initially entered into symbiotic relationships and then gradually merged with one another.[30] Consequently the 'will to life' shows itself, as Teilhard de Chardin stressed, as a 'striving for union'. Aggression – and also Bresch's hypothesis – should always be viewed and understood out of this background.

If humanity accelerated its own brain growth through battle between groups, then we must reckon that the evolutionary process favoured the more aggressive individuals. The inclination or disposition to kill could have thus found its way into biological structure within the advancing evolution.[31] The theological significance of this is that sinful behaviour promoted the growth of the brain and shaped the further development of humankind.[32] Thus we have new perspectives for interpreting the doctrine of original sin. If sin did not occur in the beginning of an already complete humanity but itself played an active role in the further course of hominization, then it becomes easier to understand why sin is ensconced in human nature itself. Therefore we can acknowledge without further difficulty that there is in the human individual 'a basic state of the natural constitution of the perverted life',[33] as Pannenberg formulates it. This means there would also simultaneously be a long history of death anxiety that left its imprint on sinful humans.

If the supposition is correct that sin has become interwoven into the natural tendencies of human life through the course of evolution, then from a theological perspective we would pose the question of the possible meaning of such an occurrence. The idea that sin was a grasping after the fruit of the tree of knowledge, and that it actually led to more knowledge, is found already in the biblical story of the fall in paradise. Also the idea that something evil can have positive consequences was already familiar to the Christian doctrine of redemption (*felix culpa*). But how is the growth of the brain to be theologically evaluated in this connection when it was both a(n) (indirect) product of sin and also belongs to created human nature? This strange phenomenon lends itself readily to comparison with the theological factor of the 'law'. In any case, the following reasons support this parallelism:

1. A more developed human brain was necessary so that humans could invent writing and produce and understand a differentiated law, as in the Old Testament.
2. As the law should help in overcoming evil, so also should the growing brain serve to regain through increasing knowledge that nearness of God which had initially been lost.
3. Although the law was good in itself, yet it served sin de facto and produced wrath (see Romans 4:15; 7:7–13). In a similar way the growth of the brain, good in itself, did not lead to greater peace among men and between humankind and God, but resulted in increasing conflicts and more conscious sinning.
4. As the negative effects of brain growth manifested themselves, especially in the growing ability to make ever more dangerous weapons, so the negative side of the law was manifested predominately in the letter that kills (see 2 Corinthians 3:6).

Consequently, we may judge the growth of the brain as theologically similar to the law. It was good and belongs to the goodness of creation, and it should have served to overcome evil tendencies through greater use of reason. But in fact sin proved so powerful that it was also able to bring the good under its power. In the course of evolution, therefore, the possibilities for evil became more conscious, greater, and more refined and ensconced deeper and deeper in human beings. This development is seen in the fact that both the growth of the brain and the law, which came later, served violence in strong measure. Most prominent among the improved tools that humans were able to produce, thanks to their growing intelligence, were weapons.

Through this connection between law and brain growth the long history of humanity's evolution to its present form bears a theological meaning. According to Paul the law had the task of training the people Israel and serving as their custodian until the coming of Christ (Galatians 3:23–25). If we utilize Paul's pattern of thought, then we could say mankind was prepared for the new truth of the revelation by the growth of the brain and the development of a differentiated capacity for knowledge. A more complex capacity for knowledge was needed in order for humans to become able to receive a word consciously and reflectively as the word of God.

Dramatic Redemption as Creative Transformation of Sinful Human History

According to the picture I have sketched, sin penetrated the natural human constitution in the course of a long history, which began with an initial fall and stretched over great periods of time. By contrast, the history of the law in Israel was a very compressed period and still more condensed was the redemption event in Christ. Even this, however, was not completed in a single action, but through a drama that played itself out in several acts and in which the decisive confrontation between the powers of evil and the power of God occurred.

Jesus began his public ministry with the message of the dawning reign of God, the announcement of God's new act of salvation occurring in the 'today' of his own time: 'Today this Scripture has been fulfilled in your hearing' (Luke 4:21). Through the new gathering of Israel the rule of God over his people would become a present reality. However, the nearness of God shining through Jesus' own work did not lead to the new gathering, but met with rejection. With this rejection God's new deed began to unfold in several more acts, and the evil provoked by the message of God's rule became the condition of a yet more radical deed of God. Jesus first responded to the resistance he met with words of judgement by which he sought to arouse the obdurate people (second act). But this proclamation had just the opposite effect and so opened a new act in the drama. The messenger of salvation and judgement was expressly and violently rejected (third act). Jesus bore the condemnation and the evil inflicted upon him by answering the violence he suffered with surrender to God: 'When he suffered, he did not threaten, but he entrusted his case to the righteous judge' (1 Peter 2:23). The judgement of God followed on Easter (fourth act) in that the heavenly Father raised the Crucified One (the 'stone rejected' by men) and made him the 'cornerstone' of a new community (see Mark 12:10 and parallels). In the appearances of the Resurrected One the executed master became present in a new way to his disciples beyond the distance of time and death. In this new presence he simultaneously awakened in them hope for his final coming. This presence of the Risen One in the Easter appearances, still stressful and anxiety-ridden as it was, became that which, though tension laden, was full of peace, thanks to the Spirit of Pentecost (fifth act). Since then, in the word of proclamation and in the celebration of the mysteries of Christ, which are conveyed and fulfilled through the ever present Spirit, the past salvation event in Christ (announcement of the Kingdom, message of judgement, death, resurrection) becomes a constantly new presence for all times.

In this briefly sketched dramatic process of salvation we see an extremely intensive compression of time; yet it is never removed from real history but comprises and includes it. With his message of the kingdom of God Jesus referred again back to the beginning of humanity. Since he as the sinless one experienced God only as he could be experienced before sin arrived, and since he proclaimed his heavenly Father as a God of boundless goodness, he thus revealed the original divine will for humankind.[34] With the message of the dawning reign of God the original promise of victory over the serpent (Genesis 3:15) was realized. Delusion, deceit, and aggression had dominated the past, so that hope to which the original nearness of God had awakened human beings could never really develop. In Jesus' life and work, however, it gained new form and power. To humans, who had fallen into evil, he proclaimed a God who especially looks after sinners, and he announced a realm in which deceit and violence are overcome through nonviolence and love of enemies. In this he not only referred back to the beginning, but also gave all latent hopes in past history a new and living form.

Yet this new hope stumbled on the hard reality of sin. The faithfulness of Jesus to his message thus made the way of the Cross necessary. However, it can be objected that this understanding of the doctrine of redemption, which relies upon the basic possibility of salvation prior to the cross and bases the necessity of Jesus' redemptive death only on the rejection of God's rule,[35] contradicts the New Testament. The New Testament clearly teaches that everything must happen as it does (Matthew 26:24, 45; Mark 14:21; Luke 24:26; Acts 1:16; 17:3). Indeed, in the Fourth Gospel John the Baptist proclaims Jesus as the Lamb of God who bears the sin of the world (John 1:29) already at the beginning, before his public ministry. Against this objection I have pointed out in *Jesus in the Drama of Salvation* that the long historical experience of the Old Testament shows how the prophetic proclamation repeatedly encountered resistance. From this standpoint the rejection of Jesus' message, although it depended on human freedom, was not accidental and surprising, but was already clearly indicated in the history of Israel. So also the way of the Cross was prefigured in outline in the concrete history of Israel, although in the inner dynamic of God's rule it was not necessary. I can now deepen this answer somewhat through the hypothesis developed here. If Jesus in his proclamation of the new reign of God referred back again to the beginning of human history, then in his message a divine will is manifest that holds unwaveringly to the original divine gift to humankind, in spite of later sins. In this regard the Cross, according to the

clear witness of the kingdom-message, was in no way
necessary. But since Jesus appeared and proclaimed God's
rule at a point in time when, over the course of evolution,
sin had long lodged in the natural makeup of human
beings, an acceptance of his message was no longer possible on a purely ethical level. Nevertheless, the kingdom-
message remained a real possibility. To realize it a
miraculous power was certainly needed, namely a faith
that could move mountains (see Matthew 17:20; 21:21;
Mark 11:22–23) and liberate and heal the human nature
that was ill and imprisoned by evil (see Mark 1:21–2:12
and parallels). This faith did not yet include the Cross but
the willingness to lose one's present life in order to gain it
through God in a new way (Matthew 10:39 and parallels;
16:25 and parallels). Also part of this faith that Jesus
intended to waken with his message was the willingness
to bear the sufferings and sins of others, as he himself did
in his healing activity (see Matthew 8:16f.). So in spite of a
long history of human sin the original will of God was not
simply out of date. Indeed, the merely ethical appeal had
become powerless in the meantime, as the fate of the
Israelite prophets shows. In Jesus, however, there came a
new possibility: the innermost dynamic of God's dawning
reign, occurring through a mountain-moving faith that
subverted the whole past history of sin so as to heal the
sickness of human nature. This interpretation of the necessity of the Cross takes into account two different perspectives that cannot be further reduced,[36] both of which
respectively encompass all of human history. It might well
be the most suitable interpretation of the passages in the
Gospels that seem so opposed to one another.

Through our hypothesis we can also conduct the judgement sayings and discourse about the wrath of God to a
more profound interpretation. In the context of dramatic
theology the judgement sayings are interpreted as self-
judgement, which means that evil deeds fall back on the
head of their perpetrators.[37] Our hypothesis, that human
sin has worked itself into human nature over the course of
evolution, would accordingly be nothing other than the

most radical consequence of the self-judgement to which God has delivered humankind. The concepts of judgement and original sin thus draw very near to one another.

The Old Testament mentions again and again the experience that humans are not judged according to the measure of their personal guilt (see Psalm 73; Job; Ezekiel 21:8f.). If the self-judgement to which God hands over sinners works itself into human nature, then we may infer that it occurs not only where a consciously evil act is done, and not only against the one who is culpable. Rather, the perversion of what is naturally human affects all of history and also besets all those who bear little responsibility for misdeeds. It can be viewed and experienced as a tragedy. When the great prophets of the Babylonian Exile simultaneously emphasize that each person is punished solely for his or her own sins (Jeremiah 31:29f.; Ezekiel 18:1–32), then this emphasizes that the experience of God in Israel was unconditionally a matter of personal responsibility. But the complaints and laments of the post-exilic period show that very often one could not determine an appropriate connection between guilt and punishment. God's judgement seemed to be imposed again and again without reason. It was inscribed in nature.

From this perspective we can shed light also on Romans 1:18–32. There Paul speaks first of all of God's wrath that is revealed from heaven on all unrighteousness of men, in order then to state that God gave them up to the lusts of their own hearts, to dishonorable passions, and depraved thinking. In biblical exegesis both statements, the revelation of wrath and the deliverance of humans to their own evil doings, were often separated from one another, although the opposite reading of Paul's text recommends itself. That is to say, the Apostle expressly stresses three times that God gave humans over to their passions because of their evil deeds. This giving over seems therefore to be the concrete form of divine wrath. Most interpreters nevertheless tended to the opposite conclusion. This may be because the giving over was usually understood too superficially and thus was unable to explain the dramatics of wrath as it was described in the Old Testament. However, since our hypothesis holds that giving over means that God gives humans over to an often cruel evolutionary process, all are delivered up to a true wrath. Only from the original perspective of the message of God's kingdom and the resurrection of the One Crucified can it be still maintained that God in himself is never wrathful.

In Romans 1:26 Paul also says that homosexuality is an effect of 'wrath' and a consequence of God's giving over. This view of the Apostle stirred up an often furious polemic in recent times. Many scholars think they can show that the homosexual tendency is inherited and therefore cannot be unnatural.[38] By means of our hypothesis it is possible to maintain both views without inner contradiction. If 'wrath' was already operative in intra-human evolution, then on the one hand homosexuality may very well be a consequence of sin at a basic level, as Paul says. Yet on the other hand it may also be an inborn tendency of that historical nature of mankind which the empirical sciences investigate and which forms also an important element for practical ethical judgements.

Finally, our hypothesis facilitates a more profound understanding of why redemption must be achieved through the death of the Redeemer. Dramatic theology holds that his being delivered to violence was the result of the inner law of sin. The first sin led quickly to fratricide and the universal spread of violence (fall – Cain and Abel – Lamech – humanity before the flood). If now the redeemer has taken on himself the consequences of this history of sin, then he must also become a victim of violence. At this point of the argument the question may certainly be raised whether God could not at the last moment have snatched his Son away from the actual power of death, as many psalms intimate (see Psalms 37:32f.; 40:3; 69:15–19) – for instance through a miraculous liberation of the Crucified One. From the standpoint of our hypothesis, however, even the death of the Redeemer was necessary. If sin was deeply etched in human nature, then evil can only be overcome if this nature itself dies and is created anew by God. The death and resurrection of Christ thus turn out to be that radical divine response of redemption which, since the faith that moves mountains could not be awakened, was necessary in order to heal the long evolutionary history of sin from its very roots. Full salvation can therefore take place only through death, and an immanent or this-worldly presentiment of this salvation is only possible where people do not simply count on their good will and their own moral efforts. To the contrary, the old self must die with Christ (Romans 6:1–11; Galatians 5:24f.) so that the new self can be born in the power of the Holy Spirit (John 3:3–8).

The process of redemption accordingly occurs as a dramatic recapitulation and victorious reversal of the long history of sin. The whole past of humanity is lived anew in the history of Israel and finally compressed in the drama of Jesus' destiny. From Pentecost on even the short earthly destiny of Jesus is again condensed and brought to genuine presence in the Spirit-inspired word of proclamation as well as in the celebration of the Eucharist.

Compression of Time and a New Understanding of Time

If the doctrine of evolution may help us deepen the history of sin and redemption in some regards, something similar may also be true regarding the compression of time. In conversation with modern sciences T. Horvath has elaborated an understanding of time according to which there is in the order of creation already something analogous to the compression we see in salvation history. He clarifies that every time runs its course on the basis of sub-times. The rhythmic movements of molecules become superimposed on the movements peculiar to atoms. The molecules in turn rise into what is inherently cell life. The rhythm of the individual organs develops over the cells; the organs are taken over by the life process of every human, in which the movements of the earth and the stars also have influence. From the modern scientific insight into the multiple overlays Horvath infers to begin with that time is to be understood as equilibrium or suspended balance of a multiplicity of sub-times. He shows further that the irreversible direction of the past into the future belongs to this suspended reality. He concludes that time is a 'balance in a multiplicity of sub-times characterized by an irreversibility measured through uniformly reversible changes pointing to a self-sublating singular event.'[39] With the reference to self-sublation Horvath indicates that even the many, seemingly endlessly recurring movements by which time is measured have an inner tendency and direction toward a goal. The atoms whirling in a molecule can fall apart. In the course of their repeated rhythms cells, organs, and living beings draw closer to death. And even the movements of the planets and the solar system, seemingly always the same, travel toward future explosions or collapses.

Out of the background of this briefly sketched understanding of time Horvath shows how the time of Jesus encompasses the times of all other humans. By his message of the dawning reign of God he, confronting the ever recurring movements of human times with God's time – eternity –, has placed a unique choice before them. Moreover, by his death and resurrection his own human time was fully taken up into God's eternity. In this way the difference was bridged between his historical time, in which he was the proclaimer, and the time after Easter, in which he was the one proclaimed. All this was possible because in Jesus Christ, as Horvath repeatedly stresses, the eschatological union of time and eternity came about[40] and so his time became the revelation of eternity.[41] As compressed time, Jesus' time encompasses the sub-times of all human beings. With this comparison Horvath does not intend to assert an identity between the manner in which the time of a living being comprises all the subtimes of its organs, cells, and atoms and the way in which the time of Christ assumes the times of all men. But he certainly points correctly to an analogy, for all humans do indeed form a body with Christ in the power of the Spirit. In this fashion it may be somewhat more understandable that the revelation of eternity in the dramatically compressed time of Christ actually includes the sub-times of all humans.[42] This inclusion of all in the salvation event can, conversely, be the standpoint from which light is once more shed on the bond connecting everyone in sin.

Corroborating Indications

Our central hypothesis is that sin penetrated human evolution and led to 'a basic state of the natural constitution of the perverted life'. For this hypothesis there is obviously no direct evidence in the tradition. But if the postulate is relevant, then already before the discovery of the principle of evolution believers must have had experiences that are indirectly in accord with the hypothesis, even if they were not able to adequately interpret these experiences.

An example for our assumption is found in Paul. In the letter to the Romans he says that the mind set on the flesh is hostile to God; it does not submit to the law, for it cannot (8:7). According to the Apostle, therefore, the law is powerless. The old self must die with Christ in order to participate in new life through the resurrection. Another question resonates in this passage, and Paul addresses it expressly in Romans 8:19–22: 'For creation awaits with eager expectation the revelation of the children of God. For creation was made subject to futility, not of its own accord but because of the one who subjected it, in hope that creation itself would be set free from slavery to corruption and share in the glorious freedom of the children of God. We know that all creation is groaning in labour pains until now.'

Whether Paul means here the whole creation including all men; the whole creation except the Christians; the non-human creation; humanity or the world of angels, is disputed since the exegesis of the ancient church until today.[43] In the most recent exegetical works the debate goes on. Thus N. Walter holds, based on the correspondence between Romans 1:18–31 and 8:19–22, that all creation clearly means sinful humanity (besides the Christians).[44] Against this E. Grässer counters with the argument that Paul speaks of an involuntary subjection, which does not apply at all to humans according to Romans 1:18–31. He maintains that the Apostle thinks especially of the animal world in speaking of the groaning creation.[45] Both Walter and Grässer cite noteworthy reasons in their arguments, and other reasons speak against both of them. The objection to Walter's position, besides the arguments of Grässer, is that in Romans 8:3 Paul characterizes sinful humanity not as creation, but as flesh.[46] Why should he have changed his use of language so soon thereafter? Against Grässer, however, is that his interpretation leads to the conclusion Paul sympathized with the animals, but not with human beings who were not Christians. Yet this contradicts his whole theology. So none of the possibilities of interpretation is satisfying.[47] Another question remains unclear in Romans 8:19–22: who subjected creation, God or Adam? On this point most exegetes agree that one cannot make a clear decision between the two possible interpretations.[48] In view of this confused situation our hypothesis does not claim to give a better interpretation of Paul's text, but it certainly proposes to interpret this very lack of clarity in a new way. Thanks to his faith, Paul has experienced 'bondage to decay' so deeply in himself and spotted it so clearly in others that he instinctively had to credit created nature itself with the transience of life, yet he was unable to express this experience conceptually without contradiction. What Paul perceived correctly, yet could not clearly express, was that effect of sin which penetrated into created human nature over the course of evolution. Therefore the creation actually sighs and waits in longing for redemption.[49] Not only human being as ethical, but also human being as creature is in need of being freed from 'bondage to decay'.

We find an analogous issue in the Church Fathers. Even prior to them Philo of Alexandria, with reference to the two reports in the book of Genesis, distinguished two creations of the world.[50] Many Fathers, for example Origen, Gregory of Nyssa, and Maximus Confessor, followed him in this, but they developed the idea of two creations in a different way. Whereas Philo, out of the background of Platonic ideas, contrasted the creation of the eternal ideas from the creation of individual concrete things, Origen made a temporal contrast between the creation of the Logoi (souls) at the very beginning and the creation of actual humans, namely the connecting of the fallen logoi with the subsequently created bodies. Gregory of Nyssa's interpretation was that God intended human being to be a heavenly creature without sexual difference in an initial, virtual creation, and with this as model all humans would form a single body. But because the Creator foresaw sin, in the second, real creation he clothed human beings with a sexual nature borrowed from the animals.[51] Similarly Maximus Confessor held that marriage was not part of the first creation. His doctrine of the double creation is different though from Gregory of Nyssa to the extent that he concluded the first humans went astray just when they were created, so that God's act of creating went on to the second creation, to the creating of mankind's sexual nature.[52] Much of what we find in this doctrine of double creation can no longer be accepted today. Its biblical starting point, the two creation accounts, are construed quite differently in modern exegesis. These accounts offer, moreover, no reason to distinguish between a non-sexual and a sexual nature of humans, for in both narratives human being is referred to as man and woman (Genesis 1:27; 2:18–25). However, our hypothesis can derive an acceptable meaning from the strange idea of the double creation, which strongly influenced Eastern theology in particular, and so must certainly speak to a genuine experience. If evolution continued after the fall into sin, above all in the growth of the brain, then the human nature that had its origin under God's influence through a 'fulguration' or through 'self-transcendence' (Rahner) from animal life should be clearly distinguished from the second human nature as we know it today. The first can be characterized as good, while the effects of sin have entered into the second, as in the opinions of Gregory of Nyssa and Maximus Confessor.

Our hypothesis also leads to a new interpretation of another theme in the theology of the Church Fathers. According to Athanasius the death of Christ on the Cross was necessary to fulfill the demand of the law. That threat of death that God pronounced already in paradise for the transgression of the law had to become reality; otherwise he would be seen as untruthful. Through his death on the Cross Christ thus had to pay the price of his life to that law, which was enacted in the beginning of mankind.[53] We find concepts similar to what Athanasius presents, although less clearly worked out, in numerous Fathers (Cyril of Alexandria,[54] Proclus,[55] Theodoret of Cyrus,[56] Hilary,[57] and Ambrose[58]). Maximus Confessor deepened Athanasius' thinking on the death of Christ by bringing it into connection with the double creation. According to him God directly inscribed the law of death in human nature because of the Fall. It consists in nothing other than the law of sexual reproduction and birth, which leads quickly to death and so exercises a tyranny in which the sovereignty of death is established in human beings, in their lust. Maximus holds that Christ has gradually overcome this law of death. First of all, thanks to his virgin birth he was not subject to the law of lust and the ownership of death. Yet for our salvation he took on the human nature that is apt to suffer and is stamped by sin. Thus Maximus applies to the Incarnation Paul's statement that Christ became sin on our behalf. In the Incarnation the Logos took on a nature marked by the law of sin. Therefore Christ must, as a further step, also suffer death, which Maximus understands as belonging likewise to the law inscribed in human nature. However, since death had no claim on one without sin, Christ was able to transform it: out of death as a weapon of the law and the judgement against nature he created a weapon against sin.[59]

If we exclude from Maximus' thought those elements connected to the view of human sexuality mentioned above, we then see how close our hypothesis is to his view of the law of sin inscribed in human nature. If intra-human evolution came about under the influence of sin, then its effects actually entered into the bodily and psychic makeup of humankind. The redemption of human beings therefore necessitated a miraculous power (virgin birth, faith that moves mountains) and a miraculous acceptance of death, by which its negating power could be transformed in surrender to God.

Remembrance Celebration and Transformative Recollection

The celebration remembering and representing the death and resurrection of Christ is central to the life of the Church (Eucharist, other sacraments). The compression of time, which was the subject above, here continues. Moreover, these celebrations show how central is the dimension of memory for Christian existence. Remembering (anamnesis) God's deeds of deliverance and petitions for the renewed favor of God in the present were always part of biblical prayer. Our hypothesis, that the human organism is a living recollection of the long history of the cosmos and the earth, provides a basis for this central structure of Christian existence in the created order itself. The memory does not belong just to intellectual activity; we ourselves as organisms are living memories.

When we turn to the subject of redemption, our hypothesis concerning the influence of sin in our organic nature makes clear that the reappraisal of earlier negative deeds and experiences also belongs to the more comprehensive memory. The Old Testament prayers often included the confession of the repeated failure of the people (Psalms 78; 89; 106; Baruch 1:15–3:8; Nehemiah 9:6–37; Ezra 9:5–15; Daniel 3:28–42). Also the New Testament kept the memory alive of the deficient faith and the failure of the disciples chosen by Jesus (Mark 6:51f.; 8:17–33; 9:33–37; 10:35–45; 14:10f., 50, 66–72). However, the Church in its liturgical prayers remembered its failure chiefly in the form of individual confession, while it scarcely confessed its failure as 'holy people'.[60] This might be why so much conflict occurred within Christendom. If our hypothesis makes sense, then the necessity of an enduring anamnesis becomes clearer, a remembering that includes both the long dark history of early humanity as well as the dark aspects of the history of Christianity. As long as important dimensions of evil remain concealed, certain deep layers of the consciousness of individuals and the Church are in danger of remaining closed to the saving act of God.

In our interaction with the past, two dimensions are to be distinguished, tradition and memory, as S. Freud in particular systematically elaborated.[61] The first takes place at a conscious level, whereas the memory lives out of the subconscious realms. Freud classified religions completely at the level of memory and saw in them the emergence of repressed earlier experiences that were transformed. Against this thesis, at least in its global form, is the fact that the Jewish-Christian history of revelation has in no way repressed the darkness in its own past. Admittedly there are also religious forms of expression that point to instances of repression. In some biblical prayers, for example, a revealing self-righteousness is reflected (Psalms 58; 109). In other prayers the wish for the destruction of enemies stands so much in the foreground that any feeling for the victims and for the speaker's own guilt is suppressed. Yet such sacral mixed forms don't belong to the central core of revelation, as R. Girard in particular has shown. Like Freud he also categorizes religions and human societies primarily at the subconscious level and interprets myths as concealments of prior violent acts and the aggressive impulse of the community. But in distinction from Freud, Girard sees in the great religions, and above all in the Jewish and Christian revelation, an impulse that moves decisively against the powerful tendency of repression. Accordingly, in the Gospels, and especially in the crucifixion and resurrection of Christ, God uncovers and overcomes the whole subliminal, violent, and repressed past of humanity. In spite of the continuing remembering of this event in the Eucharist, the truth was able to succeed only very slowly and haltingly, as the societies in which Christians live functioned according to the principle of repression. In addition, a great deal of denial and failure was also concealed in the Church itself. Nevertheless revelation generated a transforming impulse that, inter alia, has influenced human society in the form of secularization and has given a strong impetus to the emergence of the sciences.

Our hypothesis is a more detailed extension of the Girardian perspective. The basic disclosure of the underground mechanisms of violence occurs, of course, in the Gospels. At that time, however, the only concepts and metaphorical expressions available were those found in the Judeo-Hellenistic world (see Matthew 21:33–46; 23:29–39; 26:12, 1–12; 26:47–28:20). Until the ultimate consequences of these metaphorical expressions could become conceptually clearer it was necessary to have a slow transformation of human society and human knowledge through the impulse of the Gospel revelation. Girard's theory and, in even greater measure, our hypothesis would not be possible without this transformation. The hypothesis thus reckons with a hermeneutical circle of world-historical scale. Accordingly, the revelation has thoroughly leavened culture and made new forms of knowledge possible in a very slow, yet comprehensive process. Thanks to this knowledge we can now look back and grasp with greater conceptual clarity some things in many canonical texts whose metaphorical character was difficult to decipher. The great historical course of remembering/anamnesis thus leads not only to a new appropriation of the revelation, but also to a clearer understanding of its meaning and implications.

Genetic Engineering and Apocalyptic

The final dimension of our hypothesis, the future, must still be briefly addressed. Teilhard de Chardin saw all of reality in the light of evolution. This means that humankind had its origin in evolution; in human beings evolution has become conscious of itself. Teilhard even supposes that evolution will also continue beyond modern man, not indeed at the biological level but in the realm of the noosphere.[62] Teilhard could not say exactly what this step into the future would look like. He spoke in metaphorical language of a process of complexification, of unification with simultaneous differentiation. Since his death the biological sciences in particular have made enormous progress. Today we must take into account that these sciences can even set biological evolution on its way again. It is already possible deliberately to introduce new gene material into the genome of mammals. In this fashion animals with new features can be bred, and perhaps in time even new animal breeds can be developed.[63] What is technically possible for animals may certainly not be out of the question for humans. Scientists take this possibility into account in any case,[64] and if previous humans already had an active though unconscious part in the evolution of their species, as our hypothesis supposes, then a conscious human intervention would not be completely surprising.

Concerning an ethical justification of a possible change of the human genome, scientists and others point to the possibility of being able to heal illnesses.[65] That may actually be true for many cases. In fact, our hypothesis offers the following thought to consider: If the sin of human beings has imprinted their organism, could overcoming these negative imprints not only be allowed, but could it be the actual task of humanity to do so as far as possible?[66] This would certainly be an extremely ambiguous and dangerous project. On the basis of prior experiences with science we may assume that future developments would be determined especially in the interests of money and power. It is easy to imagine what the result would be if the conceivable potential were systematically exploited by dictatorships. A greater segment of humanity would then run the risk of becoming material for the putative well-being of a certain group, 'waste' or 'loss' may even be justified with the claim that a super-man or over-man is being bred. But it is not simply an explicitly dictatorial policy that is problematic in changing human beings. Everything could happen in a much more indirect way. What if it is not the human person as such, but the scientific, technical, and economic system that will stand in the middle of coming developments? A total shifting of values is certainly accepted by many as self-evident. For instance, D.B. Linke writes:

> The changing of nature grows dramatically. It is difficult to find a technological way out that does not further damage nature. Biomedical research therefore seeks ways to adapt the human organism to the changed environment. The third Copernican revolution has already fully taken hold of mankind. The human person was transformed into a subject who, as subject, developed the natural sciences for the mastery of the world; this subject has now itself become the malleable object of the various technologies.[67]

The New Testament perceives that the battle between good and evil will intensify in the time after the coming of Christ. The Revelation of John speaks on the one hand of a thousand-year reign of Christ on earth (Revelation 20:1–6), yet even more clearly of beasts which blaspheme God and confound mankind with great signs (Revelation 13:1–18). Previous exegesis interpreted the thousand-year reign as the Church and the 'beasts' as anti-Christian political empires. But could these images express an even deeper presentiment? Does the world contain a goodness that is not yet exhausted? Will the power of evil in the future take on a dimension which the biblical writer was not yet able to give an assessment, but which he had to express in metaphors instead?

These questions show that the connection between evolution, original sin, and redemption is not just a matter of interpreting the past. On the contrary, decisions on pressing current problems will be made depending on the answers given to these questions. With the catchword 'original sin' traditional theology has addressed a negative turning point in the totality of human history and with the catchword 'redemption' it has referred to the fundamental overcoming of the negative burden of the past. We cannot foresee in detail the consequences new interpretations will have in the long term. The previous history of Christendom already proves that the struggle between good and evil will likely intensify, for the European society arising out of Christendom has been engaged in an enormous venture. A glance into the future may, to be sure, tilt us rather toward a dark, truly apocalyptic outlook. But the signs of hope of the thousand-year reign and its application to the Church (which has to renew itself) may not be overlooked either. As for ourselves, if evil should have initially prevailed, the Christian perspective offers no reason to lose true hope. The starting point of the doctrine of redemption is always that God can change even what is evil into a greater and more astonishing good. 'Where sin increased, there grace abounded even more' (Romans 5:20). If a negative manipulation of human beings should occur, this could also prepare the way to an inconceivable, unexpected blessing.

Notes

1 Von Balthasar, *Cosmic Liturgy*, 201.
2 C.f. Schwager, *Der wunderbare Tausch*.
3 C.f. Schwager, *Must There Be Scapegoats?*
4 Idem, 'Neues und Altes zur Lehre von der Erbsünde' (now the first chapter of this book).
5 Idem, *Jesus in the Drama of Salvation*. This model was discussed in an interdisciplinary symposium in 1991; C.f. *Dramatische Erlösungslehre*.
6 C.f. *Evolution. Ein Kontroverse*.

7 Bresch, *Zwischenstufe Leben*, 46.
8 J. Klima, 'Reichweite und Grenzen der naturwissenschaftlichen Methode', in *Evolution*, 69–81, here 76.
9 On the question concerning the connection between freedom and the history of sin, see Schwager, 'Neues und Altes zur Lehre von der Erbsünde'.
10 'With great probability he [homo habilis] was … one of the earliest toolmakers; the oldest artifacts of the so-called Olduwan culture were discovered in 2.5 million-year-old layers at the Gona River in Ethiopia. They are still the oldest witnesses to human culture.' E.-M. Winkler, 'Stufen der Hominisation', in *Evolution*, 95–106, here 101.
11 C.f. Koltermann, *Naturphilosophie*, 213.
12 Depending on where one exactly begins the development of human beings, their brain capacity was between 600 and 1000 cm, whereas modern humans have about 1400 cm; cf. E.-M. Winkler, 'Stufen der Hominisation', in *Evolution*, 95–106; Koltermann, *Naturphilosophie*, 214–220.
13 Cf. Koltermann, ibid., 226–233.
14 Cf. Pannenberg, *Systematic Theology*, vol. II, 186f.
15 A comparison with mentally handicapped people may clarify this: 'It is important, however, to recognize and acknowledge the fact that mentally handicapped people have an intensive spiritual life and so also a prayer life. Even if their intelligence and their feelings are disturbed, they, not always, but often have a very lively and direct relationship with God. I believe a reason for that is that this relationship with God is not controlled by the intelligence, so that the handicapped person is, so to speak, exposed defenselessly to the love of God … On this subject Jean Vanier and Father Thomas Philippe have made an unintended discovery, which is that people with a mental handicap can have, despite all disturbances of intelligence and feelings, not only an intact but an especially intensive spiritual life.' Marsch, *Gottes Wege*, 119f.
16 'On the way to our destiny and in relation to it, we are not just subjects. We are the theme of a history in which we become what we already are.' Pannenberg, *Systematic Theology*, vol. II, 228.
17 Cf. Anselm of Canterbury, *Cur deus homo* 2, 10.
18 Intra-biblical considerations already show that the narrative of the fall in paradise, according to which sin consists of transgressing an express divine command, requires a New Testament reinterpretation (see the first chapter). This idea of the fall originates in Israel's faith. For it the most central situation of decision-making consists of saying Yes or No to the law of Moses. In the New Testament, on the contrary, a different perspective is found. Paul holds that the explicit law first entered after sin (Rom. 7:7–13). In the stories of the temptation of Jesus we see a situation which involves preserving the given experience and the received gift while not using it high-handedly for oneself. Regarding the good angels, Anselm of Canterbury supposed that they had remained attached to what is good without knowing possible punishment for sin (*Cur deus homo* 1, 17).

19   The kinds of behaviour that at one stage of evolution are 'good', 'adequate', or 'beneficial' may prove at the next stage to be 'bad', 'detrimental', or 'disruptive'. This can be elucidated through other examples. Thus on the level of amoebae the direction of evolution is such that each one multiples itself as much as possible. But as soon as the step to multi-cell organisms occurred, the limitless multiplication of the single cell becomes a negative phenomenon for the multi-cell organism, namely cancer.

20   R. Spaemann, 'Über einige Schwierigkeiten mit der Erbsündenlehre', in Schönborn, *Zur kirchlichen Erbsündenlehre*, 41–66, here 65. The Bible tells that God led all the animals to Adam so that he could give them names (Gen. 2:19f.). In the framework of the evolutionary theory this passage could be reinterpreted in the sense that humans have the task of leading 'animal being' beyond itself to a goal. Sin may be characterized as man remaining imprisoned in his past (see the serpent).

21   Dostoevsky, in his story, 'The Dream of a ridiculous Man', offered a helpful concept of the fall. He describes how evil began on an island which did not previously know sin: 'Oh, perhaps, it all began *innocently*, with a jest, with a desire to show off, with amorous plays, and perhaps indeed only with a germ, but this germ made its way into their hearts and they liked it. The voluptuousness was soon born, voluptuousness begot jealousy, and jealousy – cruelty ... Oh, I don't know, I can't remember, but soon, very soon, the first blood was shed; they were shocked and horrified, and they began to separate and to shun one another. They formed alliances, but it was one against another.' *Great Short Works of Dostoevsky*, 733–734.

22   Since humans are bound very closely to one another, they form at the same time a system. However, both experience and modern research show that in systems even slight deviations in the beginning –through constant reactions – can lead quickly to enormous effects. As one says in meteorology, for instance, the beating wing of a butterfly in Africa can unleash a hurricane in the Caribbean.

23   E. Voland, 'Hominisation, Homologie und Heuristik. Ein Plädoyer für den Tier/Mensch- Vergleich', in *Evolution*, 83–94, here 85, 87.

24   Numerous texts in the Old Testament reinterpret the biblical language of direct divine punishment by the idea of God giving sinners over to their own self-judgement. Cf. Schwager, *Must There Be Scapegoats?*, 53–71.

25   Cf. Girard, *Things Hidden Since the Foundation of the World*; idem, *The Scapegoat*.

26   Bresch, 'Zwischenstufe Leben', 196.

27   Ibid., 198–202.

28   Pannenberg, *Systematic Theology*, vol. II, 266f.

29   Cf. Margulis and Sagan, *Origins of Sex*.

30   Cf. W. Wieser, 'Die Evolution hat viele Gesichter – und jedes sieht dich an', in *Evolution*, 29–55.

31   Cf. Voland, *Grundriß der Soziobiologie*; Pöltner, 'Evolutionäre Erkenntnislehre', in *Evolution*, 133–146, here 145.

32   The genetic material of humans and the highest animals is almost

the same. This suggests that forms of behaviour are not (only) stored in the genes, but above all in a still largely unclarified 'epigenetic system.' Also E. Drewermann, for whom behaviour research is 'today a far better ally of depth psychology than learning theory and socialization research', accepts a 'very far-reaching, biologically grounded archetypical pre-forming of the human psyche, by comparison to which the conditions of the sociocultural environment can evoke only relatively insignificant modifications of what is common everywhere.' Drewermann, *Tiefenpsychologie und Exegese* I, 231.

33 Pannenberg, *Systematic Theology*, vol. II, 257

34 Already Irenaeus interpreted Gen. 1:26, which says that man was created in the image and likeness of God, as not merely signifying the creaturely order, but as an announcement of the covenant to come.

35 C.f. Schwager, *Jesus in the Drama of Salvation*, 29–81.

36 It is not possible to gain a higher standpoint in order to tie both perspectives into a single system (e.g., through a doctrine of predestination). It is characteristic of a dramatic theology that it intentionally rejects seeking such a higher standpoint. In an attempt like that it would see a very subtle, yet that much more dangerous temptation of wanting to obtain the divine standpoint surreptitiously in order to be able to grasp the interaction of God's action and human freedom.

37 In the Old Testament there are about 70 passages that speak of self-judgement. See Schwager, *Must There Be Scapegoats?*, 237, n. 13. Also all of the judgement sayings of Jesus can actually be interpreted in this sense. See Schwager, *Jesus in the Drama of Salvation*, 53–81.

38 LeVay, 'Evidence for a Biological Influence in Male Homosexuality'; Byne, 'The Biological Evidence Challenged'.

39 'Time is a balance in a multiplicity of sub-times characterized by an irreversibility measured through uniformly reversible changes pointing to a self-sublating singularity event.' Horvath, *Eternity and Eternal Life*, 60.

40 Ibid., 65–80.

41 'God, who is one and identical with eternity, assumes and becomes time like any created being. He becomes a balance in a multiplicity of sub-times characterized by an irreversibility measured through uniformly reversible changes. Therefore for faith time and eternity are not mutually incompatible realities as human reason would conclude. Time is not eternity and eternity is not time, yet Christ is both: time and eternity. Consequently neither eternity nor time should be considered without the other, because in Christ time became the revelation of eternity and eternity is revealed as the origin and the end of time.' Ibid., 73.

42 The idea that the time of Christ encompasses all past time is found already in Irenaeus. He holds that Christ recapitulated all events in earlier history and so turned evil into good: 'Since therefore he (Christ) summed up everything, he also recapitulated the battle against our Enemy.' *Against Heresies*, V 21.1.

43 Wilckens, *Der Brief an die Römer* II, 151. Even St Augustine commented: 'Hoc capitulum obscurum est, quia non hic satis apparet, quam nunc (Apostolus) vocet creaturam.' ('De div. quaest. 83' [*CChr.SL* 44A, 164]).

44 Walter, 'Gottes Zorn und das "Harren der Kreatur"', in *Christus bezeugen*, 218–226.

45 Grässer, 'Das Seufzen der Kreatur'; C.f. Wilckens, *Brief an die Römer* II, 153.

46 Still more clearly in Romans 7:5–25; Galatians 5:17.

47 In this open question a problem could come to the fore which remained unresolved in the Old Testament. Gen. 1:30 says God gave the animals only plants as nourishment. But according to Gen. 6:7–13 the animals belong to the 'creatures of the flesh' through which the earth has become full of violence and which God will destroy in the flood. Yet how the animals became violent is never indicated. The faith of Israel here encountered a problem which it had not the means to solve.

48 C.f. Grässer, *Seufzen der Kreatur*, 107; Wilckens, *Brief an die Römer* II, 154.

49 According to this view humans would have the task of 'redeeming' what is questionable in the animal world so that through living with God they would cleanse and overcome (see Gen. 1:28) the forms of behaviour inherited from the animal realm. Thus whatever is questionable in preceding evolution would be integrated into a more perfect unity. On account of sin, however, the old forms of behaviour gained a new, perverse dominance. So not only did the higher stages toward which evolution strives fail to take place, but a relapse occurred.

50 Philo of Alexandria, 'On the Account of the Creation Given by Moses. Nr. 16:129–135', in idem, *Works* 1. Tr. F.H. Colson, 101–107.

51 Gregory of Nyssa, 'Hom. Op. 16f.' (*PG* 44, 181A–192A); C.f. Schwager, *Der wunderbare Tausch*, 81f.

52 Maximus Confessor, 'Quaest. et dub. 3' (*PG* 90, 788AB); idem, 'amb. 41' (*PG* 91, 1305C, 1317D); cf. Völker, *Maximus Confessor*, 102–135.

53 C.f. Schwager, *Der wunderbare Tausch*, 66–69.

54 Cyril of Alexandria, 'De adorat. in spe et ver. III' (*PG* 68, 293C–296A); idem, 'De recta fide ad reginas, orat. altera 7' (*PG* 76, 1344BC).

55 Proclus, 'Orat. de laud. s. Mariae 5' (*PG* 65, 685).

56 Theodoret of Cyrus, 'In Isaiam 53:4–12' (*PG* 81, 441–444).

57 Hilary, 'In Ps. 53:13' (*CSEL* 22, 145); idem, 'In Ps 129:9' (*CSEL* 22, 654); idem, 'In Ps. 135:15' (*CSEL* 22, 723).

58 Ambrose, 'De fide 3,2,13' (*CSEL* 78, 112); idem, 'De fuga saec. 7,44' (*CSEL* 32,2,198).

59 C.f. Schwager, *Der wunderbare Tausch*, 147–150.

60 For this reason the confession of guilt and the prayers for forgiveness that the Pope and cardinals spoke on behalf of the Church on the first Sunday of Lent in 2000 were a great and important step of renewal.

61 C.f. Freud, *Moses and Monotheism*.

62 'Above all matter is not just the weight that drags us down ... In itself ... it is simply the slope on which we can go up just as well as go down, the medium that can uphold or give way ... Of its nature, and as a result of original sin, it is true that it represents a perpetual impulse toward failure. But by nature too, and as a result of the Incarnation, it contains the spur or allurement to be our accomplice towards heightened being, and this counter-balances and even dominates the *fomes peccati* [spark or tinder of sin].' From the starting point of our present moment in world history, the place of our birth, and our individual vocation, 'the task assigned to us is to climb towards the light, passing through, so as to attain God, *a given series of created things* which are not exactly obstacles but footholds, intermediaries to be made use of, nourishment to be taken, sap to be purified and elements to be associated with us and borne along with us.' Teilhard de Chardin, *The Divine Milieu*, 77.

63 Capecchi, 'Targeted Gene Replacement'.

64 'We can anticipate continued improvement in gene-targeting technology, but it has already created opportunities to manipulate the mammalian genome in ways that were unimaginable even a few years ago. To significantly aid in deciphering the mechanisms underlying such complex processes as development or learning in mammals, researchers will have to call on every bit of their available ingenuity, carefully deciding which genes to alter and modifying those genes in ways that will bring forth informative answers. Gene targeting opens a broad range of possibilities for genetic manipulations, the limitations of which will be set only by the creative limits of our collective imaginations' (ibid., 41).

65 C.f. ibid.

66 From brain damage and corresponding changes in human behaviour researchers believe they can establish which part of the brain has a particular association with social and ethical activity. C.f. Damasio, 'The return of Phineas Gage'; LeDoux, 'Emotion, Memory, and the Brain'.

67 Linke, 'Die dritte kopernikanische Wende', 63.

Chapter 3

God's Self-Communication and the 'Interchange of Freedom'

The problem of original sin encompasses several dimensions. Sin, in its intrinsic character, is part of the human dialogue with God. In its effects it concerns the entirety of human history. And as that special form of sin which is passed on by human parentage, it belongs to the natural history of mankind. The three dimensions can of course never be separated from one another, but they are nevertheless clearly distinguishable. Thus in the first chapter, human history stood chiefly in the foreground. In the second chapter we gave greater attention to the question of natural history (evolution), and in this chapter we turn expressly to consider the dialogue with God and to supernatural history.

What tradition designates as supernatural should not be (mis)understood as only an external and object-like addition to the nature of man. As K. Barth and K. Rahner have clearly shown, the self-communication of God to human beings belongs to their supernatural calling, and this self-communication demands a response stemming from creaturely freedom, which reaches down into the deepest roots of the self. The self-communication of God and the total opening up of the human self in a process of radical freedom correspond to one another. So it is that we will view the doctrine of original sin from the perspective of the question of a radical freedom. Therefore we turn in what follows to a work that sets out to understand original sin consistently in the context of a doctrine of transcendental freedom and raises the claim to move beyond contradictions in the traditional doctrine in this way.

Original Sin as Transcendental Denial

H. Hoping conceives human being as transcendental freedom, and he attempts to interpret original sin in this light as transcendental denial. He holds this in contrast to P. Schoonenberg, K. Rahner, and E. Drewermann, who, he charges, do not really think freedom through to its essence. Rather, he contends, they put it forward only as a special attribute of human being.[1] He stresses that if original sin should be a determinant of freedom, it must also be 'a determinant *stemming from* freedom'.[2] 'For a determinant of freedom that does not arise from freedom itself would eliminate the concept of freedom.'[3]

Hoping, proceeding from Kant's establishment of the concept of freedom in his transcendental philosophy and in alignment with H. Krings, discerns also the origin of cognition in transcendental freedom.[4] J.G. Fichte radicalized the task of transcendental philosophy and exposed the transcendental origin of all knowing (including self-knowledge) in the 'I am' as an absolutely original action. However, Fichte could not overcome the Kantian theory of self-consciousness because he continued with the concept of the self as a foundational philosophical concept. By contrast, Hoping stresses with Krings the relationality of all knowledge, and he understands this as transcendence with reflective structure in which the formal significance of 'transcendental' appears. One must go behind the transcendental I 'to an absolutely original transcendence from which the entire relationality of knowing, thus also the transcendental I, proceeds'.[5] This original transcendence, or the 'transcendence of transcendental freedom',[6] is not a human attribute but the condition of being human as such. It presupposes being as content and may therefore be designated as original, transcendental listening. 'The original perceiving of being is the de-cision (or un-locking) for content, that is, for being in general. This de-cision ... establishes an openness in which being can begin to exist and thus become evident.'[7] Transcendental understanding or transcendental listening does not presuppose 'a finished I as subject of understanding' but constitutes in the first place the 'being of the subject as self'.[8] It cannot be 'an event that would somehow be experienced, since it provides the very basis of experiencing self-consciousness'.[9] Yet it has the character of event because the transcendence of transcendental freedom must be understood in terms of temporality and is essentially a 'freedom of the moment and the situation'.[10] This freedom is thus in origin bound up with time, world, and history in such a way that these spheres form the space of its self-formation.

Because primordial listening ('de-cision') has an unconditioned character, the content of this understanding must itself be unconditioned and so be a form of freedom in its own right.[11] In the transcendental self-formation our self-being proceeds from the de-cision for freedom of the other (transcendental affirmation), and the 'interchange of freedom' is 'transcendentally earlier than the subject'.[12] Transcendental freedom thus understood opens up history and orients it at the same time.[13] Since, however, no historical form of freedom is able to fulfill its own freedom in its unconditional character, its original decision must transcend itself in the direction of what is absolutely unconditional. Thus appears the idea of a perfect freedom, which is not only formally but also materially unconditioned, and therefore the possibility of a revelation of God becomes intelligible.[14]

Hoping interprets the traditional doctrine of original sin on the basis of this transcendental understanding of freedom; he sees it as 'the historical character of transcendental denial'.[15] This denial does not come about within history, but is a 'primordial event of freedom in the process of constituting the human self-relationship'[16] and in the original creaturely temporalizing of freedom. On the one hand, through this denial the meaning of being, time, and history are perverted, while on the other the idea of a historical fall into sin becomes superfluous. 'In the framework of this transcendental-historical origin of sin the supposition of a singular fall at the historical beginning of human history becomes as obsolete as that of some primordial situation that preceded it.'[17]

Hoping's understanding of original sin represents a radical new interpretation of the traditional doctrine. But does he still deal with the doctrine of original sin at all? We certainly welcome Hoping's intention to consider the human person not as a given thing or as only part of pre-human nature, but as radically free being. Nonetheless, in his clarification of transcendental freedom he himself emphasizes that this freedom precedes the constitution of the self as subject and has a purely formal character. Yet we would ask whether a purely formal structure that constitutes human being, even if this is conceived in terms of event, could sin at all? Hoping himself makes a distinction between transcendental and moral freedom.[18] However, only the moral freedom of a subject that has already been basically constituted is able to sin at all, for only that subject has the freedom to make choices. The kind of 'sin', however, which is placed directly in the process of constituting human being and prior to freedom of choice,[19] must be a metaphysical occurrence, as we find more or less in the speculative theories of original sin proposed by Schelling or Tillich. Hoping deliberately attempts to distance himself from these theories.[20] Nevertheless, his view – in spite of certain differences – is very similar to them. Since he wants to comprehend the doctrine of original sin completely from the standpoint of the formal actuality of transcendental freedom, the formal actuality takes on the character of content through the back door. Though Hoping denies it, his view finally tends toward the alternative of either a pre-world fall of the soul or even an identification of evil with human being in general. The basis of this problematic alternative may, as indicated, be that a content function is ascribed to the formal reality, and the expression 'transcendental freedom' could have been the immediate starting-point for this misunderstanding.[21] Since the word 'freedom' and the expression 'transcendental freedom' touch on the idea of decision in the sense of freedom of choice, it is tempting to ascribe secretly to transcendental freedom a concrete 'de-cision' of a moral kind, although it ultimately denotes only a formal differentiation in regard to being and the moral good. The word 'freedom' used like this plays a role similar to the speech of the serpent in the paradise narrative: both became the occasion of temptation because the element of analogy, which ultimately is an element of mystery in the language used, is overlooked.

Although Hoping's interpretation of original sin leads astray rather than forward, his expositions still contain aspects which are worthy of note. The question of original sin should be pursued all the way into the process of constituting what is human. In this, however, we will probably not succeed by placing sin within this constituting process; instead we should ask how sin in the historical sense involves a feedback on that process of constituting humanity.[22] For this our point of departure has to be from the standpoint of sin that has been overcome.

Sin Overcome and Unity in Salvation

Sin is a *mysterium*, and failing freedom has no essence, as Karl Barth always emphasized, but a 'non-essence', so to speak. Sin essentially produces a false appearance: it is a lie (see Matthew 23:13–33; John 8:44; Romans 3:10–18) and thus conceals its own origin. We can therefore ascertain it only indirectly. We can shed light on it only retrospectively from the standpoint of its having been overcome; through this light it is recognizable as in a silhouette. This is why we must turn to Christ and his victory over sin to begin here.

Through his message of the imminent reign of God Jesus intended to gather anew humans, who are charac-

terized by suffering and worry. He proclaimed true salvation as the gift of God and as life in a regenerated community. But the opposition to his message soon provoked him
to use a language of judgement, and he had to speak of
hell as the last imminent consequence of humans being
closed up within themselves. In this way he revealed an
abysmal possibility of human freedom and showed that it
is impossible to avoid freedom and responsibility. Even
the most intense fellowship in the kingdom of God does
not eliminate the responsibility of each and every individual. Yet this wasn't the last word of Jesus. He was not
satisfied with announcing the fate of hell to those who
resist and fail in their freedom. As the Good Shepherd he
also went after them in their isolation in order to woo
them once again, even at the point of the furthest distance
from God – dying in his own final weakness on the Cross.
In this process he allowed himself to be hit by the collective violence of his enemies, and he had to experience that
even his heavenly Father left him alone in his final loneliness (Mark 15:34). His fate makes clear that there is a final,
unavoidable loneliness even for that creaturely freedom
which the divine love completely permeates. But from this
radical loneliness and freedom the new community arose.

Already before his passion Jesus offered himself to
human beings symbolically in bread and wine, and as he
was dying he breathed out his Spirit for those who persecuted and killed him (see Mark 15:37; Hebrews 9:14).
Through the resurrection his heavenly Father made him
the spirit-filled, imperishable principle of life for all, and
through the sending of the Holy Spirit his dispersed disciples were assembled anew in the empirical world and
brought together as the community of the Church. The
salvation announced in the message of the Kingdom led
beyond dramatic and deadly conflict to salvation in the
spiritual body of the Risen One, whose real symbol on
earth is the Church.

The language of body is more than a gratuitous
metaphor. In the letters to the Romans and the Corinthians
(Rom. 12:4f.; 1 Cor. 12:12–31a) Paul does not utilize this

metaphor to distinguish head and parts, but he understands all together as the *one* body, which is the Christ: 'For as a body is one though it has many parts, and all the parts of the body, though many, are one body, so also is Christ' (1 Cor. 12:12). In this one Christ, Jew and Greek, man and woman, slave and free are 'one' (Galatians 3:28) and form a new, complex individual[23] (corporate personality, 'Great-I'[24]). In the vision on the way to Damascus Saul experienced the inseparable unity between Christ and believers, for the Risen One asked the man who persecuted his disciples, 'Saul, Saul, why do you persecute *me*?' (Acts 9:4). And when Saul asked who the speaker was, he heard the answer: 'I am Jesus, whom you persecute' (Acts. 9:5).[25] Thus the Risen One indicated the unity between him and his disciples with the word 'I'. The converted Saul could therefore say of himself without exaggeration, 'I live, yet not I, but Christ lives in me' (Galatians 2:20).

Christian thought faces the task of understanding freedom in such a way that the radical affirmations of the unity of all in one 'person' or in a single 'I' and the unavoidable responsibility of every individual (conversion, the problem of hell, the loneliness of Jesus on the Cross) reciprocally explain each other.[26] This happens symbolically in the dramatic and sacramental events of baptism and the Eucharist. On the one hand the candidate for baptism must reform himself, yet on the other hand the baptism is administered to him and by the power of the Spirit he is completely taken into the destiny of Jesus (death and resurrection; Romans 6:3; 1 Corinthians 12:13). His ego, in as far as it desires to be self-sufficient and autonomous, must die with Christ (Romans 6:6) in order to be raised with him. The Eucharist indicates this state of affairs even more clearly (see 1 Corinthians 10:16f.). On the one hand, in it the self-offering of Jesus, even to the surrender of his life, is represented; while on the other hand, this takes place in the form of the food that those who eat assimilate into their own body. Through this unique and free self-offering the Ego of Jesus is so transformed that it becomes food which can be received and assimilated by others to the extent they are ready to give themselves over to him in death. Supreme personal decision in one's final, dying loneliness, and a total handing over to the other correspond to one another.

The dramatic destiny of Jesus and the sacraments show how the community of salvation and unity in salvation, understood in a Christian sense, arise out of an interpersonal process. This process presupposes, on the one hand, that the participants are already (partially) constituted subjects, so that they can act, and on the other hand the event has such a radical effect on them that it transforms them – indeed, they are in essential dimensions constituted anew. Jesus himself was radically transformed through the process that he initiated. The people with whom he was engaged arrested him, killed him, and condemned him so radically to passivity that it required resurrection from the dead to reconstitute him as an acting subject.[27] Similarly the disciples who initially believed in him were reduced to such a condition of disbelief by their betrayal and flight (dying with him) that a deep transformation through the appearances of the Risen One and the coming of the Spirit at Pentecost was necessary (rising again with him) to constitute them as believing subjects – and this time as truly having faith.

The traditional doctrine of original sin may be understood afresh and more deeply only when it is seen in the light of the unity in salvation of all human beings and in light of the dramatic, interactive process that leads to this unity. Since the process of redemption had such a radical and strong effect on all participants that these sinful subjects, already provisionally constituted,[28] were again dissolved, the history of original sin must be pursued all the way into the process that constitutes becoming human. Thus theories that move only in the realm of everyday experiences, or assume the Enlightenment notion of an autonomous I are bound to be inadequate.

The Historical-Symbolic Primordial Scene of Sin

The people of the Old Testament composed the narratives of the book of Genesis on the basis of their experience of faith. Accordingly, Christians have to interpret the biblical primordial history, with its account of the Fall in paradise,[29] in the light of the salvation Jesus brought us. Since Israel experienced deliverance above all in the whole people's obedience to the commands of God (Leviticus 26:1–13; Deuteronomy 28:1–14), and calamity in apostasy from these commands, it represented the first sin as transgression of an express command (Genesis 2:4b–25). The question has been raised as to what concrete breaches in the covenant history this alludes. Modern exegetes give various answers. According to L. Ligier, Adam stands for the King of Israel, Eve for the people, and the serpent for foreign peoples. As explained by Ligier, the central failure, which was transferred back to the beginning of history, consisted above all in the people's unfaithfulness to its God Yahweh, its heeding of foreign nations and gods, and the king's acceptance of this.[30] K. Barth, on the contrary, takes his point of departure from the sin of the King (Jeroboam and the two golden calves [1 Kings 12:26–33]), which gets its fundamental meaning from the golden calf at Sinai (Exodus 31:18–33:6), and so the paradise story is to be viewed in their light.[31] Others push the story of Cain and Abel up close to the paradise narrative and see the concrete form of sin chiefly in the inheritance of violence.[32]

Since the long and dramatic history between Yahweh and his people had no real centre, it may be impossible to choose between the various interpretations, and each certainly has its own justification. However, things are quite different from the standpoint of the New Testament. Here Jesus and his destiny form the actual centre and, as we have seen, salvation through him was newly and more deeply experienced, so in this light the narratives of the primordial history should be read in a new way and critically reinterpreted. But before we can venture on this attempt, we have to observe the different elements individually that provide support for our argument:

1) In the garden story the object of temptation is an external object (the fruit of the tree). Jesus, on the other hand, had first of all an inner experience of temptation in the wilderness. When he was baptized Jesus had perceived the heavens opening, to which a similar opening of his soul must have corresponded, and he had heard words through which he was touched in his final identity and was addressed by God as the beloved Son (Matthew 3:17). In the temptations that follow, the voice of temptation starts out exactly with this experience, for it twice begins with the phrase, 'If you are the Son of God ...' (Matthew 4:3, 6). Thus in the Gospels primordial temptation does not aim at an outside object, but rather at this inner experience. This experience which comes from God and at the same time seeks to endow the recipient with his own deepest identity should be preserved as a holy mystery and gift in openness for the future, but temptation aims at misusing it for secondary and selfish purposes (see also Mark 8:32f.; 14:32–42; John 6:15). If Jesus, if this is conceivable, had succumbed to this temptation, the future-directed experience given to him would have necessarily been solidified and perverted in the direction of a deceptive identity. He would have become a 'son of god' who worshipped not the Father in heaven but an utterly different power as his 'god', as the theme of the Antichrist and particularly the narrative of the two beasts in the Revelation of John (Rev. 13:1–18) suggest.

2) In the Old Testament sin immediately brings a punishment in its train which God himself usually executes.[33] In accordance with this common conviction of faith, in the primal history God himself places enmity between the serpent and the woman (Genesis 3:15), and he banishes the guilty first humans from paradise (Genesis 3:23f.). The prologue of the Gospel of John presents a very different view, as it represents the expulsion precisely vice-versa. Here God does not banish humans from the

place of salvation, but humans reject the Word of salvation that comes to them: 'He came to what was his own, but his own people did not accept him' (John 1:11). In contrast to the paradise narrative, here the direct consequence of sin is not the punishment of the guilty but the slaying of the one God sent to his own domain. Likewise, the destiny of Jesus makes clear how the expulsion concretely occurs. Although he wanted to gather the people Israel, and through it all peoples, in the name of his heavenly Father, what happened in fact was an alliance and mob action against him. Different Jewish groups, which were normally in conflict with each other (Pharisees, Sadducees, Zealots, Herodians), acted together for a moment, and even in alliance with the hated pagan power, in order to get rid of the disturbing preacher. Looking back at his fate and at the suffering of those similarly persecuted, the early church affirmed, 'Indeed they gathered together in this city against your holy servant Jesus whom you anointed, Herod and Pontius Pilate, with the Gentiles and the peoples of Israel, to do what your hand and your will had long ago planned to take place' (Acts 4:27–28). According to the New Testament the immediate consequence of sin is thus not the expulsion of the humans from the place of salvation (paradise), but their ganging up on the bringer of salvation and his execution (parable of the wicked vineyard tenants). Although the mechanism of the scapegoat alliance is not described in the Garden of Eden story, it is found in many other passages of the Old Testament. In numerous psalms the just person complains that lying, violent enemies surround him. Prophets are often persecuted by the entire populace, and Israel as a whole appears continually as victim of the many nations.[34] The primordial history should be read with new eyes in light of these accounts.

3) In the paradise story the serpent tempts Eve directly with the promise that she will be like God (Genesis 3:4). The temptations of Jesus in the wilderness by the devil were by contrast less direct. He was not, like her, immediately allured with the promise to be like God, but invited

to a false trust in God and to worship of the false god (Matthew 4:1–11 and parallels). Even more indirect was the temptation of Jesus (*skandalon*) that came from Peter, who with good intention wanted to dissuade his master from continuing on his way and therefore Jesus had to reject him as Satan (Matthew 16:21–23). At the culmination of the conflict everything happened just under the appearance of something good. In the Garden of Gethsemane Jesus probably had once more to endure inner struggles and temptations, because he knew that God can do everything: 'Abba, Father, to you everything is possible' (Mark 14:36). If this is so, why then isn't a way without suffering possible? Precisely his vast conception of God, which entailed the possibility of becoming abstract, was the last temptation for Jesus. The same held for his opponents – with the great difference that they succumbed to the temptation. They believed that they had to act as they did. They accused Jesus of blaspheming God (Mark 14:64 and parallels), and, indeed, that he was of a satanic spirit because he was only a man and yet made himself out to be God (John 10:33). The law of God demanded consequently that he be executed (John 19:7). The element 'to be like God' that is found in the paradise story crops up here again, though now not as a direct temptation but as an accusation against someone who is charged with succumbing to this temptation. Since it is the view of the Gospels that the assault of men on the true messenger and Son of God betrays what prevails at the deepest level of their hearts, this accusation reveals the normally concealed human arrogance. The enemies of Jesus employ literal adherence to traditional commands to reject the newly emerging call of God. Thereby they can follow their own underground intention to be autonomous like God and at the same time hide this perversion, even from themselves. Only in the parable of the wicked vine-dressers does Jesus openly reveal the rivalry of the tenants with the beloved Son and their desire to have their own way by seizing what doesn't belong to them, for the vine-dressers goad one another on when the son arrives: 'This is the heir. Come, let us kill him, and the inheritance will be ours' (Mark 12:7). Yet even here the vinedressers do not engage directly in rivalry with their lord, but with his son. Since God was apprehended as more and more mysterious and unfathomable in the course of the Old and New Testament experience of faith, a direct rivalry with him is no longer realistically thinkable. Therefore it took on an indirect form of which individuals were not at all aware any longer. It now expresses itself as the collective will of a humanity that high-handedly seeks to construct a world without God (cf. the Tower of Babel). It is in this context that we must interpret the seductive serpent and the devil. This requires another inquiry, which we will take up in the last chapter.

4) In the garden story Adam and Eve appear as fully constituted subjects. Only God's decree of punishment (exhausting work, pain in childbirth) and the expulsion from the garden allow us somehow to sense that in sin we encounter a process that has repercussions on all fundamental conditions of life, although the narrative can only explain this effect as an immediate deed of God, as direct divine punishment. By contrast, in the process of salvation as depicted in the New Testament it becomes clear how the sin that Jesus exposes sets an active process in motion which leads to his death in his earthly existence and to a reconstitution of his human subjectivity by his resurrection from the dead. To conceive of an analogous, though negative event in humankind's beginnings has only became realistically possible through the theory of evolution. Therefore this theory might not be an impediment to a more deeply understood doctrine of original sin, although many theologians in recent decades have thought so. From a dramatic New Testament viewpoint the theory of evolution should in fact be helpful in making clear how sin can have effects all the way into the self-formation of humans in a process of self-punishment.

5) According to the biblical primal history God first created Adam and only later – after the creation of the garden – formed Eve from Adam's rib (Genesis 2:4b–25).

Israel's exegesis, which in many practical questions influenced Paul (see 1 Corinthians 11:7–9), deduced from this narrative sequence a preeminence of the man over the woman. This view was nevertheless gradually corrected, first of all through the concrete comportment of Jesus toward women, then by the Risen One, who made himself known first to women (See Matthew 28:1–10 and parallels; John 20:1–18), and finally through the pneumatic experiences in which women also participated. From this Paul made a point of concluding that in Christ there is no longer man and woman, but in him all are *one* (Galatians 3:28).

From these five briefly sketched reinterpretations that the New Testament performs on elements of the garden narrative, a new, somewhat changed primordial scene can be conceived. This scene can obviously be intended as historic-symbolic only. That is to say, it aims at real events in the beginnings of humanity and thus intends to be more than a mere etiology; on the other hand, the primordial events can only be sketched in 'aetiological retrospection'[35] from later experiences and from the uncovering of sin through Christ, so that all historicizing description is impossible.

The attempt to sketch a primordial scene from today's standpoint must, however, take the current world view into consideration. Just as mythical traditions were reworked[36] in the biblical primordial history, so today the efforts to feel our way back into the beginnings of humanity must give the knowledge offered by evolutionary theory its full weight. Since this knowledge takes a theoretical rather than a narrative form, any contemporary historical-symbolic idea of the beginnings of mankind can be plausibly developed not in narrative but only in theoretical form.

The act of self-transcendence by which, under divine influence, humans developed out of a group of higher animals led experientially to an intensive, yet provisionally still implicit elimination of limits on the horizons of consciousness. Thus emerged the task of

gradually realizing this new human possibility in order
to explicitly constitute human consciousness as such. By
this call a mysterious Presence also summoned the first
humans to embark on a path that would eventually lead
them – through an unknown, shared future – to explicit
cognition of God and communion with Him and among
themselves. In absorbing that experience, however, the
group shied away from its mysteriousness and the
intensity of communication. Instead they heeded the
voices of their familiar (animal) past and turned the gift
they had received into a means of self-assertion. Thus
the removal of restrictions on consciousness led to a
problematic self-formation of human consciousness,
because it included experiences of fear of the numinous
and an increased tendency to violent conflicts. The
summons to communication and a common future took
the form of negative communion (scapegoating mob) in
which members of their own group became victims.

The elimination of boundaries on consciousness that came
with the development of human being as such can be
designated from the standpoint of natural science as emergence or fulguration,[37] and as self-transcendence[38] from a
philosophical point of view. Teilhard de Chardin attempts
to contrast both aspects from one another and at the same
time to coordinate them by the distinction between
tangential and radial energy.[39] Judging from the goal of
human development, which has been shown to be the
community in the body of Christ, we have to suppose in
any case that the transition from animal to human being
did not happen in a single individual, but in a group.[40]
This means at least two individuals were necessary, for in
view of the goal of emergent human being a sexual union
between a human and an animal for further propagation is
hardly conceivable.

The moments of freedom in this originary process do
not need to be fixed in greater detail. As in small children
conscious experiences and decisions can begin quite early,
even if we cannot determine precisely when free actions in

the proper sense become possible, so the analogous suggestion that the first humans made decisions without having a reflexive consciousness about them is plausible. The primary significance of inner perception in religious experiences and the lack of higher development of the brain among the first humans urge us in any case to the conclusion that the first decisions were not made by means of rational considerations, but between the feeling of a call and a shrinking back from it. Neither the consequences of rejecting it nor the impetus for this act must have been consciously known. Decisions could have been made in the heart whose consequences were not comprehensible in the head and which appeared in the reflective consciousness only much later. They were perceived there, moreover, in a falsified form. So guilt remained deeply concealed in human consciousness, which was only gradually constituted as reflective, and its entire further development took its course under the pressure of this dark burden. But just in this way the original and mysterious call also continued to have its effect and prevented a complete standstill in human development.[41]

With these presuppositions in mind we can carry out further thought experiments as to how the primordial scene might be more precisely described – thought experiments which are inspired both by theories of evolution and by elements of the Christian understanding of salvation:

First Variant: The intensive experience that accompanied self-transcendence in the moment of hominization was given during the sexual union of two animals, and the offspring was included in the movement of self-transcendence, thus giving rise to a human group. The new and mysterious experience, with additional similar experiences, should have led to a progressive illumination of the vital sphere, to the perception of an awe-inspiring mystery in the Other and to a corresponding self-formation of human subjectivity. Since this did not happen, the numinous thrill of sexual union was misinterpreted and sexuality as such was eventually 'idolized'. This variation –

retrospectively – fits very well with the fact that sexuality was already an important catalyst in the evolution of animal life and – prospectively – that in this scenario the unity of the flesh that God had intended from the beginning according to Jesus (cf. Mk. 10:6–9) and that was to become the symbol of the unity between Christ and the Church (cf. Eph 5:31f.) had already existed at the outset of humankind.

Second Variant: The breaking-in of the new illumination of consciousness that came with hominization occurred during intensive forms of common feeding. Under this influence and the after-effects of this illumination animal feeding should have been transformed into an experience of being gifted and food should have been experienced as a living symbol of the generous power granting these gifts. That version is supported – retrospectively – by the fact that feeding was an important factor of evolution and – prospectively – that in this case the high cultural importance of the human meal and the sacrament of the Eucharist would have been prefigured from the beginning.

Third Variant. While jointly hunting or engaging in a kind of 'war of the chimpanzees',[42] the unified group was struck by an awe-inspiring premonition in the face of the stricken prey or victim. This premonition could have gradually led to a change of behaviour and to a sensitivity for the inviolability of the human person as the bearer of a mysterious presence. Actually a negative development commenced, and killing itself was more and more experienced as an awe-inspiring, fascinating (= sacred) act.[43] This variation seems plausible – retrospectively – because of the role fighting has in animal behaviour, and – prospectively – because of the all-importance of Christ's Cross for salvation.

There are no criteria for choosing between the thought experiments just listed. Perhaps it is even likely that there was a process in which all three variants plus still other factors, such as experiences of natural forces, cooperated in very complex ways. Since, however, we can infer nothing more precisely, this question has to remain open. The thought experiments are intended only to clarify problem areas and indicate fields in which tendencies to evil should be overcome today. In this way we can simultaneously make clear that the reconstructed primordial scene should not be misunderstood as a historicizing representation. The intelligibility of a primal scene as a historical-symbolic narrative chiefly has to be measured by its capacity to interpret contemporary faith experiences in-depth, and to show how they resonate positively with the modern understanding of the cosmos and history. The historical-symbolic narrative can also make understandable why the behaviour of humans has so many parallels with the higher animals.[44] A genuine universal ethic – even according to many sociobiologists – contradicts what prevails in the animal realm; there are surprising parallels, however, between the behaviour of higher animals and that morality practised by most humans. This is the double morality that shows up as altruism in one's own group and as aggressiveness toward those outside the group.[45] Thanks, however, to the completely new experiences all the behavioural patterns which the failing humans inherited from the animal realm received an utterly new significance. From the morally neutral killing in the animal sphere human murder emerged on the one hand,[46] while – on the other hand – the shedding of blood took on a sacral meaning (sacrifice) and served to weld groups together. What we know about archaic cultures suggests in any case that human groups usually came together against enemy groups and in many cases offered human sacrifices.[47] There are even traces dating back about 700,000 years that point in this direction.[48]

The Self-formation of Human Subjectivity

Enlightenment thinking considered human subjects mainly with regard to their autonomy and freedom. However, since human being exists in the context of nature and is a created being, its autonomy must simultaneously be understood as one that is receptive. This aspect of human existence was largely disregarded in modern thought about freedom, although there has been at all times a very simple and clear sign that cannot be argued away by any theory: the human being is reproduced by other humans and born of a mother. The meaning of the many genealogies, which are found both in the Old and the New Testament,[49] must lie in deliberately indicating this fundamental dependence and emphasizing its significance in the context of the supernatural calling. This is not only a matter of a so-called biological dependence, for the biblical texts recount repeatedly how the parents gave their children their names.[50] Since the identity of the self is formed by the name in the framework of a culture, the name-giving emphasizes how much humans depend on one another also as subjects and communicative beings.

This basic reliance on the other should be considered even more profoundly, namely at the level of the very self-formation of the human person. In doing this it is not enough to explicate that human being has its source in transcendental freedom and that the 'interchange of freedom' is transcendentally prior to the constitution of the subject, as we have seen in Hoping. The communicative event may only be understood comprehensively when the fact that humans are born of other humans is expressly considered too. The modern world on the one hand knows a philosophy of freedom but, on the other hand, there is a scientific tradition that investigates the question of genes and heredity extensively, including their influence on behaviour (sociobiology). The connection between both aspects is, however, scarcely taken into account, although it is a constant given in daily experience that human beings by acting freely naturally procreate other human beings. For a view of reality that reckons with a divine creation, any separation between the realm of nature and that of freedom is untenable, and so from this standpoint the connection that appears in the process of conceiving and begetting is of central importance. To reflect on this more profoundly is essential for modern civilization, which on the one hand elevates freedom, while on the other hand it pushes genetics into the centre of its endeavours. If we do not succeed in putting both the philosophical and the scientific tradition in contact with one another, modern consciousness must necessarily remain schizophrenic regarding these contradictory tendencies. Since as yet there is no sufficient preparatory work available for a deeper reconciliation of both traditions of thought, the following considerations cannot fill in this fundamental gap and must remain fragmentary. In spite of this, however, some suggestions will be attempted.

As creatures human persons are complex beings, and in their self-formation they have their source in a twofold principle, though each aspect of the principle works in a distinctive way. The double principle is called form and matter by scholastic philosophy, which owes this thinking to Aristotle. K. Rahner elaborated in *Spirit in the World* that matter should not be understood as passive on the analogy of the stone that is worked or worked upon. According to the great Greek-Scholastic tradition it is a principle, and as such is genuine origin, although of a purely receptive kind. Human being, which constitutes itself out of the principles form and matter, is therefore both actively arising origin and receptive origin. In the context of the Thomistic tradition Rahner has shown further that the human can only act insofar as his own being releases empowerment out of itself and this in an orderly way, so that it can thereby return to itself. The mind arises from the ground of one's essential being, and it then releases senses out of itself. In the ground of being, however, senses are received back first of all, then the mind. The things that we recognize are perceived initially through the senses, and then they are taken up into the mind.

These briefly mentioned analyses refer to the essential structure of the human being and are obtained chiefly by analysis of rational knowledge. From a contemporary viewpoint they contain fundamental weaknesses insofar as the question of freedom is not sufficiently considered. Mainly however the earlier conviction of fixed boundaries between species and the classical view of the relationship between soul and body actually greatly curtailed reflection on the principles and thus on the self-formation of the human person. Only evolutionary theory made it possible to construe being as origin and being as receptivity at the same time in a more comprehensive frame of reference. Rahner sought to clarify the theory of evolution by means of the idea of self-transcendence, but he didn't attempt to link this idea with his anthropology in *Spirit in the World*. Also, he never made his doctrine of arising origin and receptive origin more precise in the context of genealogical relationship, although the evolutionary theory strongly suggests this.

In spite of the limitations mentioned, metaphysics, as found for example in Thomas Aquinas, has applied the doctrine of arising and receptive origin of humans also to growth and development, especially to the question of procreation and death. The result of this was not only new insights, but also some conclusions which were already seen as problematic in earlier times. Thomas understood procreation as an occurrence that flows out of the procreators (as the arising origin) and that leads in the offspring (as the receptive origin) to a gradual reception and, to that extent, to self-construction:

> The generative power does not generate just by its own power but by the power of the whole soul of which it is a potentiality. Thus the generative power of a plant generates a plant and the generative power of an animal generates an animal; for the more complete the soul is the more its generative power is directed to an effect that is the more complete.[51]

As in cognition the mind releases from itself the senses for its self-completion, so Thomas holds that in procreation the force of the soul flows into the semen: 'The active power in the semen derived from the soul of the generator is, as it were, a kind of force of the generator's soul itself. It is not the soul or a part of the soul.'[52] With the receptive origin – here the procreated – everything is the other way round, for according to Thomas 'the soul is in the embryo; the nutritive soul from the beginning, then the sensitive, lastly the intellectual soul',[53] and in this process the respective earlier forms perish '... since the generation of one thing is the corruption of another'.[54] This view that procreation begins in the soul of the procreator and leads gradually to reception of the soul in the procreated suggests that the intellectual soul is also procreated. Yet Thomas expressly denies this, which leads to the problematic conclusion that the procreative power of human parents leads only to a vegetative and later to a sensuous soul. God then directly creates the intellectual soul – so Thomas – whereby in the moment of creation the sensuous soul procreated by the parents perishes and the intellectual soul now takes over all the functions of the vegetative and the sensuous soul. Thomas was compelled to arrive at this strange conclusion because of his position that the intellectual soul in its activity, and thus in its subsistence, is independent of matter. But this position in its traditional form is difficult to hold today. Even if spiritual activity is not as dependent on language as many currents in linguistic philosophy assert, modern brain research has nonetheless demonstrated in ever new stages how every intellectual act is connected to very complex events in the brain. This research even shows that injuries to the brain suddenly change a person's behaviour and his sense of responsibility can disappear, while all other mental activities remain intact.[55] Such scientific knowledge does not lead to the disavowal of an intellectual soul only if one does not identify distinctness and independence with one another.[56] Especially on the basis of an ontology inspired by the doctrine of the Trinity, we can conceive a distinction and polarity which is in no way to be equated with independence. In this context soul and body can be thought of as really distinct, even though the soul remains in working correspondence with all bodily occurrences.

Thomas' doctrine that human parents procreate only the vegetative and the sensuous soul entails yet a further questionable consequence. He holds, as we have seen, that procreation occurs in the power of the entire soul and this power conforms to the one conceived. Therefore humans, as they procreate only sensuous souls, can in their act of procreation only be engaged in their sensuous soul. Begetting and conceiving a child would thus essentially be 'animal' behaviour, a view which in fact corresponds to the opinion of many medieval moralists. However, this stands in tension with other statements of Thomas, for example his view that a pleasurable act of conception had belonged to life in the original paradise.[57]

There is yet a third reason why Thomas' doctrine of procreation is problematic. From the independence of the soul and of the intellect from the body he infers: 'Now the body plays no part in the activity of the intellect. And thus the power of the intellectual soul cannot, insofar as it is intellectual, come from the semen.'[58] But if the power of the intellectual principle in human beings cannot reach into what is bodily and so into the semen (because of its independence of the body), then also the sexual encounter between humans cannot be an expression of mental love. This conclusion accords once more in fact with many earlier moralists, but it stands in opposition to the Pauline teaching that the love and union of man and woman are a sign of the relationship between Christ and the Church (Ephesians 5:25–33). The devaluation of the sexual encounter also runs contrary to the experience of many Christian men and women.

On account of these questionable conclusions, the doctrine of human procreation should not be oriented to a one-sided doctrine of the soul, but must be consistently developed, beginning with Thomas' basic point of departure. Accordingly, the process of procreation takes place in the power of the entire soul, and the perfection of the one conceived corresponds to the perfection of the soul.[59] Consequently a complete human is conceived out of the power of complete humans. So the act of conception should not be isolated, but should be seen in the context of all the complex biological and inter-subjective processes that lead to the development of a new human being.[60] The peculiar questions about the intellectual soul, which arose in this context and should not be ignored, can be more precisely clarified in analogy to the theory of evolution by means of Rahner's concept of self-transcendence under divine influence.[61]

The question of the self-formation of human being appears in a new light from a comprehensive concept of procreation, which includes both the whole person in his or her freedom and also an active assistance of God. The philosophical statements about an 'interchange of freedom' receive a radical and, at the same time, concrete meaning, if one considers how a new third person is constituted out of a free and loving coming together of two persons, and how the self-construction of this new person happens in an enduring, reciprocal process with those who conceive and raise him/her. The question every child asks his/her parents, whether he/she was freely wanted and loved from the very beginning, stands not only in the background of innumerable conflicts,[62] but is actually a question of basic principle. Søren Kierkegaard asks,

> Who tricked me into this whole thing and leaves me standing here. Who am I? How did I get into the world? Why was I not asked about it, why was I not informed of the rules but just thrust into the ranks as if I had been bought from a peddling shanghaier of human beings? How did I get involved in this big enterprise called actuality? Why should I be involved? Isn't it a matter of choice?[63]

These questions are unavoidable if we understand the human person as free self-formation under divine influence[64] and 'freedom as total and finalizing self-mastery of the subject'.[65] That is to say, if human being originated in a purely natural process and his or her origin were fundamentally deprived of human freedom, then all later human deeds must be understood only as variations within the preset dynamics of nature that continually produce new beings. The language of free self-formation or of total self-disposition in this instance would only be a deceptive and euphemistic description of a more fundamental state of affairs. Participation in the great undertaking of reality, as Kierkegaard calls it, does not lie in the power of any single individual. Consequently this participation can only be a matter of freedom, if the freedom of the parents who procreate is also included. If we ask a *radical* question about our freedom, i.e., if we let our question penetrate to the roots of our existence, then it appears that we can only affirm ourselves as free if we are able to rely on a preceding affirmation by other people. Human freedom is therefore constructed on the basis of the freedom of others. If that basis fails, the human person is most profoundly affected in his or her self-formation. At the root of our freedom is the Yes – or the missing Yes – of a fellow human freedom.

Procreation is, nevertheless, a very natural process that modern sciences are able to investigate and manipulate in ever more precise ways. So here one must ask with greatest urgency about the connection between nature and freedom. The modern 'dogma' of the separation of the two realms is not useful in this endeavour. The question we are addressing shows on the contrary that this 'dogma' should be placed in question. It would not even have come up if the emphasis on freedom had always been brought into connection with procreation. Moreover, new developments in medicine show that human freedom not only must face the question whether a new human being is wanted or not. Today, thanks to technical advances, one has the freedom increasingly to intervene in the individual steps of the procreation process. This is a situation, previously considered natural and unchangeable, in which the only open question was whether the natural process was or was not to be set in motion. Now, however, many possibilities for voluntary forming and manipulating are offered. Consequently, nature and freedom penetrate each other more and more. The question of the 'interchange of freedom' still remains abstract and unreal unless natural processes are included in it.

But can freedom and nature be reconciled with one another? In view of the evolutionary image whereby sexuality and propagation seem to be the expression of a blind life force, and especially in view of the fact that many children are produced out of momentary lust rather than free intention, the quest for freedom at the origins of a new life is not familiar. We can never answer it clearly if we fasten our focus only on immediate experiences. Indeed, all humans are woven deeply into a destiny, and an incomprehensible mesh of motives and experiences stamps what they do. This holds particularly true for an act that reaches so deeply into the emotions as sexuality. The question of freedom at the origins therefore cannot be unambiguously answered by empirical means. In some cases it is likely that it has to be answered in the negative, in others it must deliberately be left open. Even where it is answered positively, many critical questions remain. Even in the instance of children who are expressly wanted it is still not clear whether a new 'freedom' as such will be affirmed by this act of the will, or whether the parents have in the end completely other, more emotional and selfish motives in their desire for children.

Since parents never fully understand their own actions, the question of their own freedom is pushed back to their line of descent. The question goes back in this way from generation to generation and, from an empirical standpoint, fades into the unknown. The doctrine of original sin may be the only conceivable solution of two problems: one is the concern to radically establish the free self-formation of human beings all the way back to their origin, the other is to do justice to the experience that much that is contrary to freedom and responsibility plays a large part in the chain of reproduction. This doctrine teaches that all human action stands under the demand of ultimate responsibility, while at the same time it says that every individual human, from conception and birth on, is negatively imprinted and burdened. This is a complex doctrine, corresponding to a complex reality. It helps to understand that in the biography of individual humans there is, on the one hand, a great lack of freedom, while, on the other hand, the principal concern for a radically understood freedom is upheld. The doctrine protects the experiences of freedom against becoming openly or secretly dissolved into natural processes. If humanity has already begun in its beginning to constitute itself in its own responsibility, yet in a negative way, as the doctrine of original sin and our primordial scene suggest, then this had to become the fate of all men to come. The dimension and problem of freedom thus continue to be fully upheld, while the massive human experiences of instinctual dynamics, subjugation, and powerlessness are taken just as seriously.

Both aspects may be more closely connected through the mimetic perspective as René Girard has developed it. From this standpoint one's own striving and desiring is awakened through the desire of another that functions as a model. By the same token one's desire is drawn almost instinctively into a deadly cycle. Of course, imitation is rooted in nature, as animal behaviour demonstrates, yet it aims toward the infinite in a multifaceted process. Therefore the possibility of distance from all instincts, and with it the opportunity for a radical freedom, remains open.

These reflections on original freedom can at the same time clarify that the complex doctrine of original sin is not self-contradictory, as many assert who would sever nature and freedom. If it holds for every human that the freedom (or deficient freedom) of one's parents becomes part of one's own history of freedom or non-freedom and enters into it as an inherent factor, it would be arbitrary to assert that this linkage is broken somewhere. The chain of conception goes back to the beginning of humankind and so all human fates and freedoms are interwoven. But in view of the massive experiences of violence, oppression, and impotence, if freedom (as potential) is to become once more actual freedom, then it is necessary to overcome all those forms of paralysis and bonds of enslavement through a redoubling of freedom. Only if this is possible, will the concern for radical freedom and free human self-formation continue as more than a(n) (illusory) idea reminiscent of Sisyphus rolling his stone up the hill.

Redoubling of Freedom and the Supernatural

The doctrine of original sin is intended to interpret the contrasts of the world in which we live. It therefore presupposes a standpoint that at least intends to be free of contradiction, which is not inserted again (surreptitiously) under another name. For this reason we have to look back again at the overcoming of sin in the fate of Jesus. We have already seen that from a Christian perspective salvation occurs as invitation to community. The unity of the community is so great it can only be expressed by the metaphor-concept of a body (or a 'self'), yet in it personal freedom is increased to the highest responsibility. This is made clear from a negative standpoint in the question of hell, and from a positive standpoint it is explicated in the total self-giving of Jesus. As to the question of how enslaved freedom can be liberated and whether it is possible to pursue the question of freedom to the end, we must again consider in greater detail the latter aspect, the self-offering of Jesus.

In faithfulness to his heavenly Father Jesus walked a path that brought him not merely into opposition to his social environment but also, at the high point of the conflict, caused a fundamental tension *in himself* to burst open, as we see in his anxiety about death in Gethsemane. Moved by his spontaneous will to live, Jesus shrank back from the death that threatened: 'Abba, Father, all things are possible for you. Remove this cup from me!' (Mark 14:36a). Nonetheless he declared himself ready to take up that way, which he had begun in obedience to his Father, once again and with finality: 'Not what I will, but what you will' (Mark 14:36b). The Spirit that had led him and enabled him to hear his heavenly Father, led him beyond his own vital instincts. Through this obedience it becomes clear that the way to which he committed himself was not simply a variant within the range of existential possibilities preset by evolutionary forces and the human community. He was called beyond the humanly possible. His self-offering distanced him from the earlier path he had taken, one he had taken in freedom and whose consequences he wanted now to avoid. Yet through the Yes on the Mount of Olives that he spoke out of the deepest crisis of his life he confirmed anew all the free acts he had posed earlier within his calling and had included in his affirmation of life.

To sacrifice one's life for one's own group and in aggressive polarization of enemies is a possibility that does not demand too much of human beings, as history and the so-called 'heroic' deeds of many combatants and warriors show. Dispositions to such behaviour are already present in the higher animals and can be easily strengthened in the appropriate environment.[66] Among men there are also additional impulses that impel them not to regard their own life in battle with enemies: anticipated honour and the aspiration to gain for themselves the rival's fullness of being (see Girard). Things completely change, though, when it is a matter of not striking back against an aggressor and risking one's own life non-violently for others and even for the enemy. There is no spontaneous impulse to this kind of act, indeed the whole spontaneous will to live speaks against it, as human experience and Jesus' anxiety on the Mount of Olives before his death show.

Non-violence in the face of mortal danger and practised in loving intervention for one's enemies brings an utterly new dimension of human existence into play. Its radical challenge makes it clear that this freedom is not simply an attribute of human being by which one can choose from the range of possibilities preset by nature. Non-violence presupposes a more radical freedom. Through this freedom we can be summoned beyond our natural limits so that we may enter again into our own past history of freedom or non-freedom and thus into our entire earthly existence. This is only possible thanks to an ultimate possibility of distancing us from ourselves and from all natural powers. The behaviour of man is based on his condition as creature and prescribed by the boundaries of his nature, although these boundaries are quite open. Therefore the non-violent surrender of one's life includes a supernatural calling and capacity. Only through surrender or self-giving can we again move beyond our own deep striving – which despite of its openness remains bound to a natural tendency. The supernatural calling encompasses a free decision toward everything that human beings live out in their natural spontaneity. Since this decision gives us our ultimate identity,[67] it must take effect all the way into the process of self-formation.

Freedom of the end, or the freedom of giving one's life, as it manifests itself in non-violence springing forth from love, encompasses the question of freedom at the origin of life. If, in view of the great forces of natural aggression and the evil of human violence, there is to be a genuine and true freedom, this freedom cannot have its origin in a purely natural spontaneity, as we have seen. It must rather be based on a clear and free Yes at its own origin. With respect to Jesus, two thematic areas may thus be highlighted and should at least be mentioned here, even if they cannot be treated more completely. One is the immemorial Yes of the eternal Son to becoming a human being that must have remained present deep in the background of his human consciousness,[68] and the free Yes of Mary in the beginning of his earthly existence.[69] Neither theme initially seems to belong to the doctrine of original sin, but they are both necessary for a doctrine of freedom carried through radically. Jesus' loving and nonviolent giving up of his life was once more a re-evaluation of his entire earlier history of life and of freedom, and it had to turn against his spontaneous vital instincts. Therefore it could not be rooted in a natural process but originated in an 'interchange of freedom'. His reflective redoubling of freedom included the preceding free acts of others (eternal Son, Mary).[70]

Another conclusion for the reflection on the freedom that comes from loving non-violence follows. Whoever offers his life when under the attack of enemies makes an implicit statement about the tendencies of those who slay him. They feel they are threatened and seize upon preventive violence. But the non-violent one shows clearly by his conduct that he is certainly no enemy; indeed, his loving surrender of his life reveals that though being perceived as attacking those who persecute and kill him, he wills only the good for them. The non-violent one is thus nearer to that desire of his enemies that want something good for themselves than they are to themselves. For in attacking, the persecutors always risk their own lives as well, whereas the non-violent one, by not retaliating, protects the life of his enemies. So by the free act of the non-violent one is more in accord with the actual will to life of the violent than the latter in their ostensible freedom. This self-giving aims at separating in the perpetrators of violence their deeper intention from their aggressive impulses and at strengthening and redirecting the former. So it is that the freedom of the (non-violent) other penetrates the basic will to live of the perpetrators of violence more deeply than their own agitated, aggressive desire. In this way we can somewhat clarify how Jesus' surrender of his life redeems sinners. Through his loving non-violence he came nearer to his enemies and to all sinners than they are to themselves. They were in need of redemption because their parents and ancestors had not unambiguously said Yes to their existence, and especially to their freedom. With their new birth the loving Yes of Jesus replaces and encompasses the lacking or ambiguous Yes of their parents at their first birth.

In light of this complete interpersonal freedom of salvation, the question of sin in the doctrine of original sin can be definitely answered. There are no sins unless through willful attitudes originating in freedom. However, this freedom is not necessarily one's own. The freedom of another person can penetrate the will of a person as deeply as his/her own and thus is able to direct it as though it were his/her own freedom. As the first humans were called beyond their spontaneous life-impulse and will to live, which they shared with the animals, to unity in supernatural community, this calling also contained the task of slowly awakening and gradually furthering in one another through reciprocal affirmation a deeper attitude of will and a conscious orientation toward God, and to strengthen that in critical situations. Every will was thus essentially dependent on the free decisions of others and so on an 'interchange of freedom' or on a history of freedom. Although this history began in a negative fashion[71] the responsibility for others still did not cease. Everybody continued to be dependent on the free acts of others in the depth of their desires, yet they received a negative imprint. Because the calling of God, as we can retroactively infer from the salvation in Christ, intended from the beginning the entirety of human history, it remained valid in spite of sin. Humanity, however, did not begin its history with positive responses to this call. Instead, we have transmitted primarily negative imprints, which penetrate even into the will. Thus we are born in original sin.

Notes

1 H. Hoping, *Freiheit im Widerspruch*, 49.
2 Ibid., 35.
3 Ibid.
4 Ibid., 235–240.
5 Ibid., 237.
6 Ibid.
7 Ibid., 238.
8 Ibid.
9 Ibid., 239.
10 Ibid., 242.
11 Ibid., 242–245.
12 Ibid., 244.
13 Ibid., 254.

14 Ibid., 255–258.
15 Ibid., 260–269.
16 Ibid., 261.
17 Ibid., 263.
18 'Transcendental freedom is the authority beyond appeal and the inner criterion of moral freedom, as well as of the individual conscience.' Ibid., 244.
19 If the full consequences of Hoping's account were drawn out, not only original sin but also redemption would have to be transferred completely into the realm of transcendental freedom. This is actually suggested by many current interpretations. This, however, would render obsolete not only the fall in the historical beginning of humanity but also the deed of redemption within history by the actual man whom 'we have looked upon and touched with our hands' (1 John 1:1), Jesus Christ. Thanks to a fortunate inconsistency Hoping avoids this conclusion.
20 Ibid., 270–276.
21 One must also ask whether Hoping's claim that original sin – ostensibly against the entire tradition – is to be conceived as a determination *out of* freedom, is more than a verbal trick that denotes the self-constituting process of the human spirit by a new word, even if the word is freedom. Moreover, the tradition has certainly never understood the *voluntas ut natura* to which it imputed original sin as nature in the objective and pre-human sense. It knew about the self-constitution of human nature (*principium*) and its formal actuality (*intellectus agens*). To be sure, modern thought, as Hoping rightly emphasizes, has explicated far more clearly than the earlier tradition that the formal actuality is dependent not only on the constitution of objective knowledge, but also and above all on intersubjectivity. That is to say finally it is dependent on the interchange of freedom. This insight should become fruitful again with regard to the problem of original sin.
22 In applying the analyses of transcendental freedom to the problem of original sin Hoping mentions creation only quite briefly (ibid., 261f.) and without sufficiently elaborating on the consequences of this doctrine for an entire view of human being. By contrast, the scholastic tradition, above all because of the doctrine of creation, interpreted man as constituted not only by spirit but likewise by matter, and so it understood the actuality of spirit from another standpoint as also a reception. In addition to the doctrine of creation the results of modern sciences (e.g., brain research) now also suggest an especially clear emphasis on this receiving aspect.
23 The 'I' in the Psalms means both the individual and the embodiment of a group or an entire community; c.f. de Fraine, *Adam et son lignage*.
24 Mühlen, *Una mystica persona*, 3.32, 4.07.
25 Because of these biblical passages there is a long theological tradition which designates Christ and the Church 'as if one person'; see the doctrine of totus Christus in Augustine ('Ps. 142, 3' [*PL* 37, 1846]; 'Ps. 26, II, 2' [*PL* 36,200]); Thomas Aquinas: '... ita tota Ecclesia quae

est mysticum corpus Christi, computatur quasi una persona cum suo capite, quod est Christus.' (*s.th. III*, c. 49a. 1 c.); on the double subsistence of Christ cf. Congar, 'La personne "Eglise"'.

26 Mühlen speaks in this connection of 'one person in many persons'. Cf. *Una mystica persona*.

27 In light of this reciprocal reconstituting of the subject we should note also the free Yes of Mary that was empowered by faith in the coming bringer of salvation and first made possible the birth of this bringer of salvation.

28 This holds not only for the sinful subjects who were the opponents and disciples of Jesus, but even of his existence in the flesh, for he bore the 'likeness of sinful flesh' (Romans 8:3).

29 K. Rahner adheres to the historicity of the fall; idem, *Foundations of Christian Faith*, 106–114; idem., 'The Sin of Adam,' in idem, *Theological Investigations* 11, 247–262.

30 Ligier, *Péché d'Adam et péché du monde* I, 232–286.

31 Barth, *Church Dogmatics* IV/1, 423–432, 437–445, 453–458.

32 C.f. N. Lohfink, 'Wie sollte man das Alte Testament auf die Erbsünde hin befragen?', in idem, *Zum Problem der Erbsünde*, 9–52; Haag, *Ursünde und das Erbe der Gewalt*.

33 C.f. Schwager, *Must There Be Scapegoats?*, 53–71.

34 C.f. ibid., 91–108.

35 Rahner, 'The Sin of Adam', in idem, *Theological Investigations* 11, 247–262, here 249.

36 A comparison with Ezekiel 28:11–19 may provide concrete evidence as to what older mythical materials were reworked in the garden story. C.f. Duff, et al, *Murder in the Garden*.

37 Lorenz, *Behind the Mirror*, 29–35, 167.

38 C.f. Rahner, 'Christology within an Evolutionary View of the World', in idem, *Theological Investigations* V, 157–192, here 163–168.

39 'At the end of the Tertiary, psychic temperature in the cellular world had been rising for more than 500 million years. At the same pace, from main branch to main branch, layer to layer … nervous systems continued to become more and more complicated and concentrated. Finally, on the primate side, so remarkably supple and rich an instrument had been constructed that the step immediately following could only be made if the entire animal psyche were to be recast and consolidated on itself …. Through an infinitesimal 'tangential' increase, the 'radial' turned around and, so to speak, leaped infinitely ahead.' Teilhard de Chardin, *The Human Phenomenon*, 113.

40 C.f. Rahner, 'The Sin of Adam', in idem, *Theological Investigations* 11, 247–262, here 252.

41 Human development initially advanced very slowly and was tied to the further growth of the brain. Only with homo sapiens did a more independent cultural development begin. Perhaps it was first in this later phase that language was fully formed. C.f. M. Donald, *Origins of the Modern Mind*.

42 C.f. Goodall, *The Chimpanzees of Gombe*.

43 C.f. Burkert, *Homo Necans*.

44 C.f. Voland, 'Hominisation, Homologie und Heuristik', in *Evolution*, 83–94; idem., *Grundriss der Soziobiologie*.

45 'An ethic corresponding to our ideals is unquestionably 'far from nature', while the actually practiced 'moralities' come considerably closer to our nature.' Ch. Vogel, 'Gibt es eine natürliche Moral? Oder: wie widernatürlich ist unsere Ethik', in *Die Herausforderung der Evolutionsbiologie*, 193–219; cf. De Waal, *Peacemaking among Primates*.

46 C.f. Vogel, *Vom Töten zum Mord*.

47 C.f. Colby, *Blood Sacrifice*; Lanczkowski, *Die Religionen der Azteken, Maya und Inka*; Tierney, *Zu Ehren der Götter*; E. Genée, 'Eine menschliche Tragödie vor 27,000 Jahren. Altsteinzeitlicher "Jahrhundertfund" in Mähren', in *Die Presse*, March 28/29, 1987 (Spectrum Wissenschaft, X).

48 In 1995 in Atapuerca (Spain) remains of human bones were found which are about 700,000 years old and which, according to the judgement of those who uncovered them, suggest cannibalism because the flesh was scraped from the bones with tools. C.f. Beardsley, *Out of Food?*

49 See Gen. 5:1–32; 10:1–32; 11:10–32; 25:12–18; 36:1–43; 46:8–27; 1 Chron. 1:1–9, 44; Ezra 2:1–2, 63; Matt. 1:1–17; Lk. 3:23–38.

50 See Gen. 4:1–25; 21:3; 25:26; 29:32–35; 30:6–13, 18–24; Lk 1:57–66. Only in quite special cases is it stressed that the name comes ultimately from God or is changed by God. See Gen. 17:5; Matt. 1:21, 25; Lk. 2:21.

51 Thomas Aquinas, *Sum.Th.* I q. 118, ad 2; cited according to *Summa theologiae* (vol. 15), 149.

52 *S.th.* I q. 118, a. 1, ad 3. Ibid.

53 *S.th.* I q. 118, a. 2, ad 2 Ibid., 153.

54 *S.th.* I q. 98, a 2; ad 2. Ibid., 155, modified.

55 C.f. Damasio, et al, *The Return of Phineas Gage*. More recent investigations apparently even show that the neurohormones oxytocin and vasopression facilitate caring, faithfulness, and love and when the corresponding hormones are lacking these forms of behaviour decline. C.f. K. Sharpe, 'Oxytocin Makes the World go Round: Love Affronts the Divine', in *Scient and Spirit* 7/1 (1996), 10.

56 For a critique of naturalism, which would like to reduce spiritual phenomena to physical and chemical processes, see Runggaldier, *Was sind Handlungen?*

57 C.f. Thomas Aquinas, *S.th.* I q. 98, a. 2, ed 3. Cited according to *Summa theologiae* (vol. 13), 157.

58 Ibid., *S.th.* I, q 118, a.2, e. *S.th.* (vol. 15), 153.

59 The understanding of conception opened up from a philosophical perspective can be pursued empirically to some extent. If sociobiology points out that among animals and humans not only physical structures and bodily characteristics but also spontaneous ways of acting have been inherited, then conception must have an effect even in psychic dispositions.

60 C.f. Tomatis, *Der Klang des Lebens*; idem, *Neuf mois au Paradis*.

61 C.f. K. Rahner, *Hominisation: The Evolutionary Origin of Man as a Theological Problem*, 93–101.
62 What is treated in depth psychology by different names – for instance, the Oedipus complex – may still usually be a camouflage of the deeper questions about free affirmation in the beginning of life.
63 Kierkegaard, *Repetition*, 200.
64 Anselm of Canterbury, inter alia, shows the centrality of the concept of self-formation for Christian thought. He finally rejects a redemption based on divine compassion because it belongs to human dignity that evil, which has its origin in the inner freedom of man, must also be overcome from within this very freedom.
65 K. Rahner, 'Theology of Freedom', in idem, *Theological Investigations* VI, 178–196, here 183.
66 C.f. Markl, 'Evolutionsbiologie des Aggressionsverhaltens', in *Aggression*, 37; also Ch. Vogel, *Vom Töten zum Mord*.
67 See the distinction between spiritual subject and person in von Balthasar, *Theodramatik* 2/2, 185–210.
68 On the mediation between the immemorial eternity of the divine consciousness and the historical human consciousness of Jesus, see von Balthasar, *Theodramatik* 2/2, 151–185.
69 The freedom of Jesus and the freedom of Mary are connected through an 'entangled hierarchy' (Dupuy). One or the other stands in the foreground depending on one's viewing point.
70 In contrast to myths, which narrate how gods had sexual intercourse with human women or even raped them, the Gospels emphasize the free Yes of Mary in the virgin conception. C.f. Girard, *Things Hidden since the Foundation of the World*, 220–223.
71 That sin became part of human reality from the beginning corresponds not only to the church doctrine that all humans are in need of redemption, but is suggested also by the following consideration: if human beings had responded in utter faithfulness to the gift received in their first appropriation of experiences that made them human and thus in the constituting of their consciousness as human consciousness, they would have been constituted as a new community of salvation. If that had occurred, however, it would be difficult to discern why this condition of salvation, once attained, had not been more clearly preserved in humanity and why it could not at least be more unambiguously detected in the deeper levels of our consciousness.

Chapter 4

Human Self-Reflection and Universal Responsibility

The doctrine of original sin must be based essentially on the Bible and church tradition. However, the reception and understanding of a Christian doctrine in a given period depends to a considerable degree on how it is related to the world view that is dominant during that period. Is the doctrine's deeper structure compatible with that world view? Does it function as a constructive challenge, or does it merely appear as a vestige of an earlier, outmoded world view? In view of these problems we have attempted in the preceding chapters to engage in a thorough exploration of a new understanding of imitation (mimesis), of evolutionary theory and of questions associated with procreation. Already in the introduction, however, we saw that the essential difficulties with the doctrine of original sin, which began with the Enlightenment long before Darwin, originate in the 'dogma' of modernity (Latour) that holds that nature and freedom (history, social order) must be separated. Since this separation has again become problematic in light of the most recent research, we deliberately left the question open as to whether and how far we could follow that theory or 'dogma' of modernity. In the preceding chapters a clear answer has emerged, which I want to summarize and then proceed to make it more precise through an explicit series of reflections on the connection between evolutionary theory and the 'dogma' of modernity.

The Organism as Memory

The theory of evolution initially made accepting the idea of a first human couple being responsible for the whole history of human sin seem implausible for many.[1] However, the same theory also indirectly had another and quite different effect, namely that the Enlightenment separation of the eternal truths of reason and the contingent truths of history was rendered problematic and out of date. According to evolutionary theory, accidental events may permanently imprint an organism and enter into its structure or into its 'essence'. Evolutionary theorists speak therefore of 'frozen accidents'.[2] Out of this background every organism can be understood as a living memory, which preserves countless accidents, bifurcations or 'decisions' in the course of cosmic and biological evolution and passes them on. Accidents presuppose, of course, a common structure for which the contingent event is either meaningful or meaningless or harmful. Conversely, however, the accident can also change common structures and make a determinative imprint on them for the future. The universal or the structure on the one hand and the particular or the accidental on the other hand are therefore not separate realities, but both are bound together by a 'tangled hierarchy' (Dupuy).

Not only the body and its functions should be seen as a living memory but also the spontaneous reactions and forms of behaviour of animals. Even normal dispositions of our conscious human behaviour turn out to be 'remembrances' that were imprinted by earlier stages or accidental occurrences in the evolution of the organism. Of course, these traces of earlier occurrences are not stored up and transmitted in a conscious way, but in the gene pool.[3] They show how particular events can enter into the nature of an individual.

If the organism is understood in light of the evolutionary theory as living memory, there are few objections against the Christian doctrine of original sin from this point of view. If it is part and parcel of evolution that individual events are preserved and transmitted, it is not implausible any more that negative decisions from the beginning of human life are being passed on until today. Certainly there is an essential difference between those many 'decisions' within evolution which directly affected the gene pool and moral decisions at the beginning of humanity. For this reason we have attempted to show, on the one hand, that moral decisions could have had at least a long-term effect on the gene pool; on the other hand, we have explicitly dealt with the question of freedom and the supernatural calling of all humans in connection with the theory of evolution. Thus the doctrine of original sin, in spite of its obvious peculiarity, enters into a positive resonance with the evolutionary world view, for it posits that events long past continue to have effects as an enduring heritage in us. Whether we are dealing with more than a resonance depends of course on whether the hereditary transmission that affects the gene pool can be brought into an inner connection with the imitation that influences behaviour.

Propagation and Imitation

The Council of Trent says of original sin that it is transmitted through propagation (procreation) and not through imitation.[4] The continued effect of negative behaviour through imitation is easily accessible to modern thinking. Yet the inheritance of a moral quality is scarcely accepted. Due to the modern separation of freedom (sin) and nature (propagation), this idea could only be seen as a mythological amalgamation of categories that have nothing to do with one another. But this suspicion of mythology at work was gradually rendered questionable in the course of our investigations. According to Girard, deeper imitation precedes reflective knowledge and it absorbs the influence of models in 'quasi-osmotic immediacy'.[5] This biological metaphor for the description of imitation or mimesis indicates that the latter is deeply rooted in nature and should not be seen in opposition to it. Tomatis shows further that imitation begins already in the mother's womb. The influences the fetus absorbs from its mother affect its further growth and especially the development of its brain. This influence begins already at conception. Finally, genetics shows that conception is only possible because the male and female gametic cells create copies or imitations of themselves, which can then fuse, and also growth ensues through a continuous copying or imitation of information in the fertilized ovum.

From conception, through growth under absorption of sensuous impressions, to imitation of moral acts, there is thus a continuous process. Imitation is completely grounded in natural processes and nature proves to be a communicative development from the very beginning, a development which gradually opens up to freedom. Procreation and imitation should therefore no longer be played off against one another. Yet, the question of freedom requires further clarification.

Freedom and Preset Nature

Christian tradition has always understood man as a creature of freedom, even if the Augustinian doctrine of predestination made the Western understanding of freedom problematic in part. But the concrete possibilities of action were very limited because freedom was perceived in the context of an order which was preset by an unalterable human and extra-human nature, which was in its turn grounded in the free creative will of God. In accord with this view, one usually also regarded social institutions as previously given by nature and thus as directly or indirectly given by God.

Within western history the struggle between Caesar and pope in part brought the preset order into question. The long-standing crisis between Church and political authority made the Reformation possible, which caused a deep rift in western society. This opened new ways in which the natural sciences and Enlightenment thinking could originate and gradually develop. The theoretical separation between body and soul (Descartes), and somewhat later between nature and freedom, untied thought on freedom from the bonds of nature for the first time, and at the same time turned nature into an object that could be manipulated at will. This development initially had consequences primarily in the social realm. In place of trust in the political authorities established by God, the idea of self-determination by the peoples (democracy) appeared, and in the toil of work one saw no longer a punishment decreed by God for original sin (see Genesis 3:17–19), but the possibility for the self-realization of one's own life and for the improvement of mankind's future (Marx). Progress in science and technology finally led to the gradual substitution of machines for many forms of human labour and to new forms of worldwide communication. In this way expanded windows of opportunity and previously unknown possibilities of creative action were developed.

However, the devices humans produced (machines) exerted feedback effects on them in complex ways. People imitated these as new models in their thinking and began to conceive of the human body according to the model of machines. So humans were no longer simply conducting research but they became the object of investigation and manipulation. The effects of research on humans appear most clearly in the increasing possibilities for changing one's nature through genetic manipulation. There is now a direct connection between theoretical insights into evolution and the practical possibility of altering one's genetic inheritance.[6]

What humans earlier thought most definitely to be preset, the environment and their own bodies, turns out to be a product of a construction process in which they themselves can intervene, at least subsequently, and they can do this ever more strenuously. The preset is thus no longer untouchable, but becomes something provisional that can be formed and changed. To be sure, this possibility does not hold for every individual person, for whom most things remain simply given, now and in future. Yet it certainly holds for human society as a whole, which created these modern possibilities and pushes them continually further. In earlier times there used to be a dialectic between individual and society, but in the meantime a third reality has appeared, technology, in which many already see the decisive subject of history.[7] Through technology nature is more and more integrated into the realm of human action, while men are molded according to the demands of the technological world. Already in our day there is talk of a 'third Copernican revolution', whose aim is not to make nature serve man but rather to adapt the human organism to a changed environment and social order. 'The human person who has turned into a subject and who, as subject, developed the natural sciences for the mastery of the world has now become the changeable object of technology.'[8] The separation of nature and freedom was thus from the very start only a theoretical separation, which in reality led to a previously unknown interpenetration and fusing of nature and history and set in motion a process whose outcome we cannot yet perceive. We are thus within a 'tangled hierarchy' that is becoming ever more universal: on the one hand, humans form society and create technologies so as to master the processes of nature, while on the other these processes and technologies form and master their human 'masters' more and more. What used to be nature, increasingly becomes the objectification and materialization of free decisions, which in their turn are subject to the increasing coercion of processes imposing their own more powerful order.

The philosophical tradition of the western world has always seen human freedom in connection with the human ability to return to oneself (*reditio in seipsum*). This capacity remained, however, very formal because of the limits preset by nature. Karl Rahner, referring to modern thought and Christian experience, has expressly emphasized that freedom is not simply an external human capacity by which man can choose between different possibilities. To the contrary, freedom concerns his entire existence and is a 'total and finalizing self-mastery of the subject'.[9] It is 'first of all "freedom of being". It is not merely the quality of an act and capacity exercised at some time, but a transcendental mark of human existence itself.'[10] 'By the fact that man in his transcendence exists as open and indetermined, he is at the same time responsible for himself. He is left to himself and placed in his own hands not only in his knowledge, but also in his actions. It is in being consigned to himself that he experiences himself as responsible and free.'[11] Rahner holds that this transcendental freedom has to execute itself through concrete objectifications throughout the full length and width of the space-time of historical existence. This occurs above all through humans taking an evaluative stance toward their own history of freedom by interpreting it and thereby endowing it with its final meaning. 'Freedom always concerns the person as such and as a whole. The object of freedom in its original sense is the subject himself, and all decisions about objects in his experience of the world around him are objects of freedom only insofar as they mediate this finite subject in time and space to himself.'[12]

Rahner developed his doctrine of freedom chiefly in light of Christ's total surrender of his life and in regard to the Christian task of deciding about one's own salvation or damnation. However, he also referred to the modern possibilities of self-manipulation: 'What is new in this issue is therefore not that man is *faber sui ipsius* [maker of himself], but that this fundamental constitution of man is manifested historically today in a totally new way. Today for the first time man's possibility of transcendental self-manipulation irreversibly takes on a clear and historically categorical form.'[13]

The word self-manipulation could suggest that these modern possibilities should on principle be judged negatively. But if freedom is the total and finalizing self-mastery of the subject, then this can hardly be true. In fact, the modern possibilities of self-manipulation provide the anthropology of total self-determination with an empirical meaning. As long as the environment, other people, and one's own body were understood as fixed and preset by nature, a strange distance remained between transcendent freedom in its openness to the absolute and the self's concrete acts of execution by means of very limited objectifications. Only when much of the preset material could be understood as objectifications of prior history and prior instances of freedom, did self-mediation become more comprehensive; a complete self-mediation could then become conceivable when humans become able to take a stand toward their entire earlier history. Biological research is at present occupied with fully decoding the human genome, and in a few years it will have attained this goal. When this occurs, human nature will not only become more transparent, but it will become possible for humans to engage in a new way with their entire past. Everything that has been built up in the process of life over hundreds of millions, perhaps billions of years is opened up to their access. With the possibility of changing our inheritance from the past, new dimensions for the future also open up. Thus an immanent possibility of total self-determination emerges. Even if immense dangers are bound up with this potential self-determination, nonetheless the new possibilities and tasks are commensurate with the Christian understanding of freedom as total and finalizing self-mastery.

The newly accessible ranges of freedom were obviously not available to humans before, yet they were already addressed in a historical-symbolic fashion in the Jewish-Christian history of revelation. This occurred not only in the narration of original sin, but also through the eschatological-apocalyptic oracles of judgement and through Jesus' unique surrender of himself for all of us in an apocalyptic context. The intention of the history of the fall in paradise was to make clear that phenomena such as oppression, the hardship of labour, and death, which earlier must have seemed naturally or mythically determined, must be judged differently from a biblical point of view: the apparently natural is to be interpreted as the consequence of prior human failure. Likewise the eschato-logical-apocalyptic oracles of judgement intended to establish a connection between human sins and the entire course of history, which to most men and peoples appeared to be determined by nature or fate. In the context of its own time the Bible could of course speak to this question only in a form of historical-symbolic metaphor and only for faith could it be understandable in some fashion.

However, the transformation processes that were mean-while awakened in the world by the Christian message led gradually and through complex stages to the point where today the issue in question has become a concrete object of knowledge. We can now establish empirically that freedom and the human potential of transformation extends into areas previously thought to be predeter-mined. From this standpoint the doctrine of original sin is thus anything but an outdated concept. In fact it proves to be a fundamental, though largely symbolic emergence of a problem which only now has taken on an immediate empirical dimension. The preset, human and extra-human nature, is the product of an earlier history and earlier bifurcations, and present decisions will become what is preset for coming generations.[14]

At the same time this insight makes it evident that freedom cannot be completely understood either from the standpoint of the isolated subject nor from that of the I-Thou relation, but must be seen in the context of human society and history in their entirety. This way all objectifi-cations of freedom become preconditions for other free acts, which in turn are the preconditions for future deci-sions. The long and complex process of the self-construc-tion of human nature and human society, which hitherto has proceeded unconsciously for the most part, has now become self-reflective. Individual self-reflection, accessi-ble to earlier human individuals within certain limits, has developed into a comprehensive process of self-reflection, which can only be fulfilled by humanity as a whole and in view of its final destination.

Since the end indicates something about the beginning, one may infer from the contemporary and imminently foreseeable possibility of free intervention in our genetic inheritance that already, in the self-construction of this inheritance, there were potentials for bifurcations (accidents), and that these potentials became, on the first level of self-reflection, authentic freedom. A retroactive freedom, which is possible from a standpoint anticipating the end of history, consequently suggests an openness in all evolution and an analogous freedom in the beginning of humanity.[15] In this regard it makes sense that freedom in its radical form as total self-determination cannot be a matter pertaining just to the individual or any group, but is a task of all mankind. All individual attempts toward self-reflection and freedom must complement one another toward an all-embracing self-reflection in which humanity intervenes in its own nature and determines itself with regard to its future and final destination. Viewed in this way, the doctrine of original sin no longer comes across as an odd curiosity in today's world. Together with the eschatological-apocalyptic oracles of judgement and the doctrine of the universal redemptive death of Christ it proves in fact to be the first and decisive articulation of that universal process of self-reflection and self-determination moving toward finality which now has become an empirical challenge and task. But if freedom is a universal process, it also becomes clear that each individual subject is more determined by the free acts of others than by his or her own self-determination. Freedom turns out also to be an affliction, something that the traditional doctrine of original sin has always known.

We are clearly not in a position to evaluate more precisely how far the already foreseeable possibilities of transformation or manipulation will actually extend into the future and how they will be used. The historical-symbolic narratives of the Bible certainly intimate significant possibilities, which should at least arouse us in these days to thought experiments in order to prepare ourselves for developments that could occur. In the book of Revelation the time up to the end is seen predominantly negatively and is described as an anti-Christian reign by means of two beasts. The first beast embodies political power, while the description of the second is that it has the appearance of a lamb but speaks like a dragon. It thus resembles the Church, the creature of the lamb, but it represents something quite different. The second animal serves the first one, erects an image for it, and possesses quite extraordinary powers: 'It was then permitted to breathe life into the beast's image, so that the beast's image could speak and could have anyone who did not worship it put to death' (Revelation 13:15). In this prophecy it is striking that the second beast not only pretends to possess miraculous power and so leads men astray, but it is actually able to breathe the breath of life into the dead image. It therefore has at its disposal quite extraordinary powers and imitates precisely what God did in the creation of the first humans (Genesis 2:7). How the biblical writer could come to the point of ascribing such powers to an idolatrous force may remain open for now. In the modern context, however, his prophetic utterance at least gives rise to the question of whether the sciences, with their instinctive quest to imitate the Creator, could in fact succeed in becoming the 'creator' in his stead. Looking from the standpoint of the Revelation of John we cannot, in any case, exclude this possibility from the outset. In this prophetic thought experiment the sciences should by no means be associated unilaterally with an anti-Christian regime. In an earlier chapter I considered as a hypothesis and thought experiment the quite different possibility that modern genetics might succeed in removing negative elements that had entered the genome through sin in the course of human evolution. The sciences appear to be an extremely two-edged sword that can lead to utterly new forms of both good and evil.

According to Revelation the anti-Christian character of the second beast consisted particularly in the fact that it would lead all inhabitants of the earth to worship the image of the first beast, and it kills all who don't comply.

If the sciences should one day succeed in creating life, evil would lie in the pressure humans felt to worship the work of their hands. They would hardly be able to see any longer that the power of the second beast finally comes from God.

What the sciences will be able to achieve in the near or distant future, we do not know precisely or at all. But from a biblical standpoint we cannot exclude the possibility that humans, by means of their self-transformation, will become able to intervene and penetrate more deeply into nature, as we can realistically foresee at the present time. Even the idea that humanity might one day encompass even what was formerly simply given, nature and the cosmos, and at least change its direction, may no longer be rejected a priori.[16] The 'dogma' of the modernity, which would separate nature and human history and which so deeply influenced modern theology, thus loses any profound basis.

'Evil' in Evolution

The question of how one should judge evil in an evolutionary view of the world greatly occupied Teilhard de Chardin,[17] and he became convinced that the doctrine of original sin should be construed out of the background of the laws of evolution.[18] Since evolution, in this view, strives gropingly from multiplicity in pursuit of unity, there are tendencies toward backslides that inevitably occur. 'In such a system, which advances by tentative gropings, the laws of large numbers make it absolutely inevitable that every step towards order is paid for by failures, by disintegrations, by discordances: the proportion of these depends upon certain cosmic constants which it is impossible to determine, but to which it would certainly be useless to claim to fix a priori an upper limit beyond which one could say that the world was corrupted or evil.'[19]

Modern knowledge of genetics has led still a step

beyond what was available to Teilhard in his time. It shows that relapses and disintegration are not simply unavoidable. Errors in the reproduction of the genetic programme now prove even to be necessary for progress to occur: 'The most perfect capability of replication is, however, its "only-almost-perfection". Without imprecision, i.e., without accidental errors, any development would be impossible. Errors of replication and subsequent selection of "fitting" changes are the motor of the growth of organic patterns.'[20] Besides errors in genetic replication great catastrophes, such as those that killed off about half of all living beings 250 million years ago[21] or that led to the extinction of the dinosaurs 65 million years ago, prove also to be important steps on the way toward human beings. It was very unfortunate for those immediately affected, but it had a positive effect in evolution.

This view is compatible with the Christian doctrine of creation and has great resonance with the doctrine of redemption. That is to say, if a free creature (human being) is to become possible, the world must fulfil a double condition. There must be great regularity in it so that the free creature can find its way and orient itself through the recurrence of similar or like experiences. The laws of the world must, however, have simultaneously a certain openness and indeterminacy. Though this may lead easily into accidents and catastrophes, it in turn makes possible real, free decisions on the part of the creature without a suspension of the laws of nature.[22]

Modern insights which can be summarized by the catchword *symbiogenesis* furthermore show that not only accident was a motor of progress. Evolution also required a process of 'unification'. Precursors of cells completely coalesced and so enabled genuine leaps in evolution,[23] even if many unsolved problems still remain for us with regard to macro-evolution.[24] Also, sexuality was quite significant, since through it distinctive genetic material was repeatedly fused and combined anew.[25] Alongside accident, which tended in a destructive direction, there were consequently strong forces of unification at work in evolution. This does not simply refer to physical and chemical forces. Animals that mated, struggled for food or defended their territories always did this without thinking of their genes or the corresponding chemical reactions. They reacted in this way because they were governed by corresponding drives. Drives were thus a decisive force in evolution. If animals were only physical-chemical machines, it would have been all the same to them whether they were dismembered (became extinct) or not. An evolution of life can only exist where there is also a drive to live, as seen in the behaviour of animals that fight for their existence and survival. Where, however, self-assertive drives are at work, interaction necessarily comes about: cooperation, competition, and fighting. Life in the animal realm offers precisely this picture: besides forms of complex cooperation there is a continual struggle for survival. This is especially clear among those animals that are closest to us humans. So it is that among certain species of apes sexuality serves not merely for reproduction, but also for lessening of conflict, indeed for 'reconciliation'.[26] In the same vein we find here precursors of human battle which means that fighting not only a matter of momentary self-defence but of long-term 'planned' destructive action against enemy groups.

For our immediate sensitivity, the natural struggle for life can seem brutal and totally 'evil'.[27] But against this negative impression one has to consider first of all, that the struggle for life itself has a goal and serves the function of self-control.[28] Moreover, besides the struggle there are likewise forms of cooperation which are even more numerous. Above all, however, the problem appears in a completely different light if we look again at nature from the standpoint of human freedom. Freedom – understood as possibility of choice – presupposes, as we have already seen, a dimension of openness and accident in pre-human nature, and thus also the possibility of negative developments. Self-determination (freedom of being) belongs also to freedom in a deeper sense, and in nature this corresponds to (evolutionary) self-development. The concrete expression of this self-development is the life-drive[29] with its manifold forms of cooperation and struggle. If the image of the watchmaker does not dominate our understanding of creation, but rather the image of a true creator who through continuous influence confers on the creature the ability to own his own being and engage in his own actions and self-development, then the deeper meaning of the life-drive becomes clear.[30] It turns out then to be the necessary precondition and the root out of which freedom may develop.

We have already mentioned that Teilhard wanted to understand original sin in light of an evolution that proceeded groping and struggling. In dependence on ecclesial tradition he designated relapses within evolution as 'the tinder of sin' (*fomes peccati*[31]) or as the provocation to sin, and in this connection he interpreted original sin as the actualization of the sparking of this tinder: 'The specifically human Fall is no more than the (broadly speaking, collective and eternal) actualizing of this 'fomes peccati' which was infused, long before us, into the whole of the universe, from the lowest zones of matter to the angelic spheres.'[32]

Now if the actual sparking of this tinder of sin had been 'absolutely inevitable' in the human realm, as a quotation of Teilhard we referred to earlier could suggest, speaking of true freedom, and thus also of sin, would be invalid. Yet since it is this very freedom that endows the life-struggle in nature with a deeper meaning, such a conclusion would destroy any explanation for the hardship within evolution. If, on the contrary, the destructive tendencies within evolution are understood only as a stimulus of sin, and if original sin is interpreted in this frame of reference, then both the specific character of sin is preserved and its rootage in pre-human evolution is clearly seen.[33] From this point of view we also realize that the concept of original sin is anything but an exotic idea. It, in fact, enables us to conjoin antithetical aspects of our contemporary world view and experience. On the one hand it maintains the concern for freedom and just in that way lends deeper meaning to the evolutionary world view. On the other hand it explains why forms of behaviour we feel are evil in the animal realm can reappear among us humans in sharpened form: in the animal realm they are actually natural, but in the human realm they are evil precisely because they have their origin in freedom as well. They may not be minimized or excused because of our animal past.

Universal Responsibility and Redemption

The concept of solidarity is a central element in modern humanistic and ethical thought. This concern already took a particularly radical and universal turn in *The Brothers Karamazov* by F.M. Dostoevsky. In this work the seventeen-year-old, severely ill Markel, brother of the Elder Zosima, finds life to be like paradise in spite of a burning fever. He says to his mother, 'Mother darling ... there must be servants and masters, but if so I will be the servant of my servants, the same as they are to me. And another thing, mother, every one of us is guilty toward all men, and I more than any.' His mother asks how he could have sinned against all men. Markel answers, 'Mother, little heart of mine ... my joy, believe me, every one is responsible to all men for all men and for everything. I don't know how to explain it to you, but I feel it is so, painfully even. And how is it we went on living, getting angry and not knowing?'[34] E. Lévinas has often cited the sentence, 'Every one is guilty toward all men, and I more than any', and he sees in it a central element of his own ethical philosophy.[35] Starting from a radical personalist thinking, Lévinas advocates an 'ethics of heteronomy that is not a servitude, but the service of God through responsibility for the neighbour, in which I am irreplaceable'.[36] The true I is 'the one who, before all decision, is elected to bear all the responsibility for the world'.[37]

This view is relevant to our reflections on original sin and redemption insofar as it poses the question of freedom. Here we are not dealing with an isolated and so-called 'autonomous' subject,[38] but one understood in the framework of all humanity and thus in the context of universal responsibility. However, a perspective such as this is not at all self-evident today, and the concept of a universal partaking in guilt and responsibility must face up to a massive challenge. The largely dominant thought about system thinking and the naturalistic positions that wish to interpret life solely as a matter of physical and chemical processes scarcely allow a place for true solidarity. Moreover the multifaceted experiences of the autonomous workings of the modern world give rise to the impression that human society has become transformed into a huge machine.[39] It is no longer free decisions that seem to determine the world, but constraints of the system.

Against this tendency of thought and feeling, it may be objected of course that it is precisely a new development within the 'world-machine' which again raises the question of responsibility. Modern society has – in multiple ways – created the possibility of self-destruction and thus has placed the most urgently vital alternative before mankind. In view of this overwhelming fact that is evident to everybody who wants to be well informed, human beings can scarcely assert with conviction that they have no responsibility. Rather the question must be raised in the opposite way: is the responsibility facing them not too great, so that it demands too much of them? Lévinas' ethical philosophy brings up exactly the same question. How can the human being actually bear responsibility for the whole world without breaking down under an unbearable burden?

H. M. Enzensberger grants a central place to this question in his study *Aussichten auf den Bürgerkrieg* (Views on Civil War). He describes how modern mass media confront us daily with so much misery, injustice, and violence in the world that we are no longer able to truly expose ourselves to all these impressions but must protect ourselves inwardly. He therefore draws the conclusion that there is no longer any infinite universal claim upon us. The idea of a universal responsibility would only make sense if conjoined with the idea of being all-powerful like God.[40] But this would be pathological arrogance. For him it is therefore time 'to take leave of moralistic fantasies of omnipotence'[41] and to familiarize ourselves with the concept of limited responsibility.[42]

Enzensberger's enquiry should be taken seriously, for the narrative of the fall in paradise shows that the attempt to be like God actually belongs to the core of the story of sin. Since this attempt, as we saw in the previous chapter, does not have to appear directly at the forefront, it can easily be concealed behind a pious or high ethical demand. Isn't the idea of universal responsibility just such a deception? Isn't this the appearance of a high ethic that covertly claims the status of being like God?

Before we proceed further into this question, we must briefly consider whether the same temptation occurs today in other ways. Nietzsche posed this question in his usually brilliant and simultaneously naïve manner with brutal frankness. In *Thus Spoke Zarathustra* he has his hero speak to his friends: 'But to reveal my heart entirely to you, friends: *if* there were gods, how could I endure not to be a god! *Therefore* there are no gods.'[43] It would be unbearable not to be the highest or greatest. There must be nothing beyond man. Instead, the latter becomes the new creator, and so he must have the heart to create the 'Overman': 'Once you said "God" when you gazed upon distant seas; but now I have taught you to say Overman. / God is a supposition; but I want your supposing to reach no further than your creating will. / Could you *create* a god?–So be silent about all gods! But you could surely create the Overman. / Perhaps not you yourselves, my brothers! But you could transform yourselves into forefathers and ancestors of the Overman: and let this be your finest creating.'[44]

The departure of God led in Nietzsche's poetic fantasy to the human being who is creative creator. Doesn't an actual feature of our social order today correspond to this

dream from the nineteenth century? Though the social
order will hardly attempt to create the Overman in a
straightforward fashion, it certainly intends more and
more to improve man, as he has been so far, through
conscious interventions. We have already seen that
modern society is self-reflective. It more and more stamps
and forms its own members and not merely on the cultural
plane, for it even interferes in their very organisms.
Admittedly people today – to use again Nietzsche's
language – are certainly only the 'parents and forebears' of
man to come. If, however, science should succeed in creating artificial life, which on the basis of the Bible cannot be
excluded a priori – as we have seen – wouldn't men understand themselves as the true alternative to the creative
divine will? Would the creative will of the humankind that
had become the Overman not take the place of the former
Creator God?

The most profound problem is that we don't stand
before coarse alternatives, but before distinct possibilities
which – on the surface – are very close to one another, yet
in actuality lie worlds apart and thus call for a very subtle
and spiritual gift of discernment. In the light of evolution,
especially in the light of the radical mandate of freedom
contained in the Christian message, one cannot reject out
of hand the tendency of humans to re-make themselves
and to assume a new attitude toward evolution and
cannot judge it as sheer mimicry of the creative work of
God and as satanic. But at the same time we cannot overlook the fact that the self-reflective process of modern
society imitates man in particular, insofar as he is a physical-chemical organism. So this tendency inclines more and
more toward substituting the living person, this feeling,
suffering, rejoicing, and therefore incalculable creature,
for another that is more controllable and thus more
predictable. This being would perhaps blend in even
better with the (ant colony) state, but this means it would
have largely lost its spiritual dimension.[45] So today we
face not only the possibility that humanity is brutally anni-
hilating itself, but we also see a tendency emerging that

humans would do away with themselves in a much more subtle and 'peaceful' manner: by transforming themselves and worshipping this process as a divine creation.

Since we now recognize such tendencies, they summon us to a correspondingly great responsibility. With that we have, however, arrived where our reflections already were. The problem has only got worse through the new sphere of questions. Humans are, on the one hand, challenged to a universal responsibility for themselves and the future, while on the other hand they seem completely overwhelmed by this responsibility. We face a dilemma, though not a hopeless one. The new dilemma corresponds precisely to the one that Anselm of Canterbury already pointed out nearly a thousand years ago in his doctrine of redemption (*Cur deus homo*). Starting from cultural and religious concepts of his time, he advanced through different stages of deepening thought to a radical concept of freedom in which he emphasized human dignity and defined freedom as the mandate 'to act out of oneself'. This resulted in the conclusion that humans themselves must rectify the evil that they have perpetrated through sin, but at the same time they are unable to do so. However, Anselm did not stop at the dilemma, but he drove his conclusions relentlessly further. Regarding this impossible obligation human beings must either despair or there must be a God-Man who as human does what humans must do and also, as God, is able to do it. We are compelled to an analogous conclusion today. If we do not intend to despair and become inwardly resigned because of the magnitude of the problem, we have to hope for deliverance.

Already in the preceding chapter theological arguments led us to the conclusion that the problem of sin can only be adequately comprehended by looking back on it from the salvation in Christ, the overcoming of sin. Now the secular problem of modern society has led us to a similar result. As long as we approach the problem of evil solely from our human perspective we get lost in a world of contradictions. Problems and challenges appear before our eyes, and we immediately see that we will never be equal to them. The orientation and trust in the meaningfulness of our lives can be sustained only if we are allowed to place our hope in redemption.

But how is redemption to be understood with respect to the problem as sketched? Since modern society has become self-reflective to a radical extent and since the most pressing problems appear in this context, redemption too must be understood as self-reflective in some manner or the other. Only in this way will it have healing effect in the 'wounds' of modern society. A dramatic soteriology[46] would probably do justice to this challenge. It would highlight first of all that the biblical history of salvation began with an orientation toward those fruits of salvation that were likewise important in an analogous fashion in the animal realm. Just as territory and progeny largely determine behaviour there, so the covenant of God with Abraham begins with the promise of land and descendants. From this point of departure a dramatic history proceeds gradually through ever new experiences and disappointments to a radical transformation of the original idea of God and so also to a new understanding of the original promise. From a later standpoint the beginning takes on a completely new meaning. Within this process of transformation and self-reference Jesus himself initiated a self-reflective process with his proclamation of the nearness of God's reign. What he initiated through his message was soon out of his hands. It developed effects on its own power and soon its reverse effects hit him with their full weight. But this reaction did not throw Jesus off his course. He used this very massive and violent backlash to live out the ultimate consequences of his own message. He gave himself nonviolently for those he sought to win, though they collectively expelled him. The only means still at his disposal was that in dying he entrusted his case to the heavenly Father and Judge in whom he had placed his hope from the beginning. The Father did not, in spite of Jesus' experience of abandonment, leave him to his fate, but awakened him to new life and elevated him to his right hand. Together they sent that Spirit who continued the work begun on earth and who at the same time retroactively clarified that Jesus' entire work of salvation, indeed the whole creation, had begun in the power of this Spirit.

Faith in a redemption understood in this way liberates us first of all from desperate attempts, bound up with fantasies of omnipotence, to find a simple recipe enabling us to get a better grip on the enormous problem of modern society. Living out of this faith, it suffices to build our trust – in the discipleship of Jesus – on the nearness of the true God, to keep track of the world process with spiritual discernment, and in doing so to trust that faith itself will initiate its own process affecting the world. It may well be that something important might get out of control, have a contagious effect, backfire on us, and once more destroy positive beginnings. But if the beginning is actually the result of faith in the God who is near, we may hope that this God will awaken new life out of the collapse of our efforts and through his Spirit establish once again beginnings that we cannot foresee. So on the one hand, much of the world process can be integrated anew into the community of faith thanks to the profound guidance of the divine Spirit, and the negative autonomy of the world can at least be broken up piecemeal. If anti-Christian tendencies nevertheless dominate the world and the apocalyptic beasts still largely prevail, which is quite possible, then there is still the hope that godless regimes will destroy themselves in the long run. Above all, however, we know in faith that true and complete salvation is promised to us only through death, as Jesus' way shows us, as eternal life with God. Salvation in a Christian sense can only be expected in passing through mortal conflicts.

The 'we' of which I have just spoken is the community of believers in Christ, the Church (and the churches). It is called to understand itself as an alternative community, and as such it must not be conformed to the autonomy of this world. The community of Christ only remains true to its vocation and meaning as long as it publicly presents a clear alternative, and at the same time avoids false conflicts. Since the self-reflective process of modern society, which reaches deeply into nature and the human organism, may not be judged negatively by the Christian doctrines of creation and redemption, we can no longer deduce ultimate norms for those trusting in the God who is near from a Nature which is preset and ostensibly eternally the same.

Natural justice has not become questionable simply due to social changes. Nature itself has been drawn into the comprehensive process of creative self-construction, as God intended regarding his free creatures, and so it is subjected to change. The norms of the alternative community can consequently be only those given us in the biblical revelation. The directives of the Sermon on the Mount seem to be crucial, for they sketch the new life in the imminent reign of God and thus in the alternative community. This goal, however, is always by far, indeed decisively, ahead of the way of life that the concrete ecclesial community is able to live out. The Sermon on the Mount is both goal and critique of what is actually lived and can be lived out in a Christian way of life. Therefore it spurs on the church community, not to fall back on past experiences so as to set itself against the forward-pushing, self-reflective process of human society, but to lay hold of the forward-looking possibilities of the kingdom of God so as to engage in critical discussion with ever new experiences in world society.

In the reciprocal process by which the community of believers builds itself up we have to discover the basic tenets of the Sermon on the Mount ever anew, understand them more precisely, and experience them as enhancing our life. Only out of such experiences can we evaluate in each case what is reasonable for the faithful in a given situation and what exceeds their powers. The experience of powerlessness is and remains essential to Christian life. It alone preserves the community of believers from pride and enables them to know existentially that they are dependent on God's guidance in all things. It gives them clear knowledge that they themselves, as long as they live on the earth, continue to need redemption.

Notes

1 So, e.g., B.K. Schmitz-Moorman, on the basis of the work of Teilhard de Chardin, believed it was finally necessary to conclude: 'that a doctrine of original sin, which originates in the sin of the primal ancestors, has been falsified by the knowledge of the evolutionary reality of creation, thus it cannot be represented as meaningful in our world.' Schmitz-Moorman, *Die Erbsünde*, 239.

2 Proceeding from the 'probabilistic and opportunistic character of the evolutionary event', one means by this term 'an ungraspable ensemble of accident and necessity. Even the rarest occurrences can in this way be determinative of future events in which the enormous ability of the organism to grow plays the role of its own reinforcing agent. Francis Crick coined the word "frozen accident" in this connection.' P. Sitte, 'Facts, Factors, Concepts, Consequences', in *Evolution*, 9–28, here 22.

3 Every individual being represents 'the evolutionary past, which is manifested in the gene pool and the different forms of consciousness'. Meyer, *Evolution und Gewalt*, 42.

4 C.f. Denzinger-Hünerman, 1513.

5 Girard, *To Double Business Bound*, 89.

6 Modern insights into the DNA-chain have brought about deeper understanding of evolutionary theory and enabled it to make a definite breakthrough. Precisely through these insights, however, we have simultaneously created the practical preconditions for arbitrary manipulations.

7 C.f. K.P. Liessmann, 'Die Technik als Subjekt der Geschichte', in *Wissenschaft und Verantwortlichkeit*, 1996, 83–97. Today one speaks also of history as having become a mega-machine and humans as post-historical animals of the species homo sapiens. Cf. Niethammer, *Posthistoire*.

8 D.B. Linke, 'Die dritte kopernikanische Wende. Transplantationsmedizin und personale Identität', in *Ethica* 1 (1993) 53–64, here 63.

9 Rahner, 'Theology of Freedom', in idem, *Theological Investigations* VI, 178–196, here 183.

10 Ibid., 184.

11 Rahner, *Foundations of Christian Faith*, 35.

12 Ibid., 38.

13 Rahner, *The Experiment with Man*, 205–224, here 213.

14 How freedom and the 'laws' of nature are related remains a mystery for the time being. For our problem, however, it suffices to show that already through both research in natural sciences and technological developments freedom and nature reach ever more profoundly into one another. All natural scientific *theories* are inseparably bound up with the scientific and technological *action* of men in the sense of an 'entangled hierarchy'.

15 Also in the Bible the narration of the fall in paradise probably achieved its definitive character only when the postexilic faith-perspective of Israel turned to the future and the end of history via eschatologic and apocalyptic thinking.

16   Because the sciences today try to find their way back not only to the beginning of life, but to the beginning of the cosmos (as in the theory of the big bang), F. Tipler now believes he is able to calculate that human life in the future will extend into the whole cosmos and even influence the further development of the universe (*The Physics of Immortality*). This view may be for now – in spite of the mathematical calculations connected to it – only a fantasy. Yet it indicates that the modern sciences never understand themselves just as theoretical efforts, but always also as instruments of intervention and change. The look back to the beginning of the cosmos thus almost necessarily awakens the notion of human intervention, which was also bound to affect the whole cosmos.

17   Because Teilhard de Chardin accepted a *radial* energy in evolution, i.e., a goal-directed power of union, his view was rejected by many natural scientists. Due to the newly discovered elements in the theory of evolution (symbiogenesis), his view has gained a new plausibility. C.f. Galleni, 'How does the Teilhardian Vision of Evolution Compare with Contemporary Theories?'

18   C.f. Teilhard de Chardin, 'Introduction to the Christian Life', in idem, *Christianity and Evolution*, 151–172, here 162–163. Against the traditional doctrine of original sin, which traces every evil in the world back to Adam, Teilhard expressed this opinion: 'Original sin, taken in its widest sense, is not a malady specific to the earth, nor is it bound up with human generation. It simply symbolizes the inevitable chance of evil (Necesse est ut eveniant scandala) which accompanies the existence of all participated being.' 'Fall, Redemption, and Geocentrism', in idem, *Christianity and Evolution*, 36–44, here 40. – On account of such statements in particular the thought of Teilhard was for a long time viewed with suspicion by the Church.

19. Teilhard de Chardin, 'A Mental Threshold Across Our Path: From Cosmos to Cosmogenesis', in idem, *Activation of energy*, 252–268, here 147.

20   Bresch, *Zwischenstufe Leben*, 110.

21   C.f. Erwin, 'The Mother of Mass Extinctions'.

22   Affirming both conditions does not signify a contradiction. The modern state of physics makes this more intelligible than previously. In the 18th and 19th centuries many believed that a total determinism would be the result of the physics of Newton. This view was in fact already false because an entire world view cannot be deduced from physical formulas. (C.f. H.-D. Mutschler, 'Die Welterklärung der Physik und die Lebenswelt des Menschen', in *Urknall oder Schöpfung?*, 43–62.) In the last century, however, the development of physics has made it clear that interpretations which go beyond physical formulas are unavoidable. Processes that can be described only with non-linear equations show that already small differences in the initial conditions, which the human mind can never determine more precisely, may lead to great changes in our world of experience. This physical knowledge permits a twofold interpretation: (1) One can hold that factors which we humans

cannot possibly control determine everything. The physical world in itself would then be purely deterministic. Such an assumption would no longer be knowledge of the physical but belief about the physical. (2) One can assume that nature in itself has a certain indeterminacy. Because of our experience as free beings this interpretation is one we can more readily accept. The indeterminacy in nature is then the place beyond which free decisions can take effect in the material world. C.f. Polkinghorne, 'The Nature of Physical Reality'.

23 C.f. P. Sitte, 'Evolution – Fakten, Faktoren, Konzepte, Konsequenzen', in *Evolution*, 9–28, especially 20–22; de Duve, 'The birth of Complex Cells'.

24 C.f. J. le Fanu, 'Doubts about Darwinism', in *The Tablet*, 2 March 1996, 290f.

25 C.f. Margulis et al., *Origins of Sex*.

26 C.f. de Waal, *Peacemaking among Primates*.

27 C.f. Schneider, *Winter in Wien*.

28 Since evolution does not follow deterministic rules, but accident plays a substantial role, complex mechanisms of self-regulation are also necessary so that order and life may develop and endure. In the realm of the living the struggle for survival between the different species, groups, and individuals is certainly a central element of self-regulation.

29 The talk of 'egoistic genes' is very misleading, for genes are chemical information. This language is correct to the extent that for evolution single individuals don't count. The central thing is the life force of a population that manifests itself in the single individual and that is reproduced through their genes.

30 On the philosophical-theological question of how accident may be reconciled in the inner world of humans with goal-directedness from the perspective of God, see R. Schwager, 'Rückblick auf das Symposium', in *Evolution*, 161–174, especially 167–171.

31 C.f. Denzinger-Hünermann, No. 1515.

32 Teilhard de Chardin, *Fall, Redemption, and Geocentrism*, 36–44, here 40–41.

33 The Greek Church Fathers already referred to a *twofold* root of the evil that was overcome through Christ: the refusal of human freedom and the frailty of a creature that was created out of nothing.

34 Dostoevsky, *The Brothers Karamazov*, 301.

35 Lévinas, *Otherwise than Being, or Beyond Essence*, 146.

36 Lévinas, *Outside the Subject* (cf. Note 4, 36), 35.

37 Lévinas, *On Thinking of the Other 'entre nous'*, 60.

38 From the beginning poets – in contrast to philosophers – have perceived how problematic the idea of the autonomous self is. C. Bandera shows that almost at the same time Descartes sought to base human cognition in a new way on the self-certainty of the ego, the great poets (Cervantes, Calderón, Shakespeare, et al.) demonstrated in detail how easily humans can get lost in dead-end situations through instinctive imitation, which leads them into destructive rivalries. Bandera, *The Sacred Game*.

39 C.f. Niethammer, *Posthistoire*.
40 Enzensberger, *Aussichten auf den Bürgerkrieg*, 74.
41 Ibid., 86.
42 C.f. Rorty, *Contingency, Irony, and Solidarity*.
43 F. Nietzsche, 'On the Blissful Islands', in *Thus Spoke Zarathustra*, 110.
44 Ibid., 109–110.
45 C.f. Büchele, *Sehnsucht nach der Schönen neuen Welt*.
46 C.f. Schwager, *Jesus in the Drama of Salvation*.

Chapter 5

Who or What is the Devil?

The Book of Wisdom identified the serpent in the garden story with the devil (Wisdom 2:24), and the theological tradition has followed this view. The question of original sin and evil led us also to the theme of apocalyptic thinking and the anti-Christian powers in which the devil or Satan plays a considerable role. Today many Christians are also concerned with this problem. Above all, numerous popular theological writings deal with the end of time and describe in dramatic images the battle between the kingdom of light and the kingdom of darkness, between the angels of God and the great Adversary with his demons.[1] Many even believe they can figure out Satan's strategy against the Church.[2] The question of original sin and evil can therefore not be treated with care without considering the question of the devil.

All humans know from immediate experience that there is an overwhelming evil that one cannot do anything about by good will alone. Thus the figure of Satan is thrust upon many believers. The history of Christianity shows, however, that belief in the devil served not only to render overwhelming evil understandable, but could also itself be the occasion of satanic aberrations. Because of the belief that one had to fight the devil, innumerable humans – particularly women – were groundlessly persecuted as witches, tortured, and killed. Friedrich von Spee, who as priest confessor accompanied many alleged witches to their execution by burning at the stake, describes in his

Cautio criminalis a terrifying picture of the structure of these trials. If suspicion fell on someone through envious talk, slander, or forced confessions, then this person could not escape. Whatever the accused did in self-defence, everything was construed against him or her and led inevitably to burning at the stake. The system of the trials had a satanic logic and, by torture and a fallacious theology of Satan, it produced itself the proof required for condemnation. Hundreds of thousands, perhaps millions of innocent people were put through a grinding mill from which there was no escape. The system of justice which intended to combat the activity of the devil was itself devilish to the highest degree.

This bitter experience of history proves that belief in Satan is anything but harmless. If evil turns out to be particularly satanic in the very battle against Satan, one must reckon with many subtle deceptions and projections in this domain. There is of course an old Christian saying that the cunning of the devil consists in making humans believe that he does not even exist. But in the witchcraft trials he seduced human beings into seeing him almost everywhere. The devil thus seems even more cunning than the language of Christian wisdom assumes. Bitter experience shows in any case that there is a way of fighting against evil by which it is nourished more than ever and gains increased effectiveness.

The witch trials had far-reaching consequences in the history of the western world, for they gave a strong impetus to Enlightenment thought, which considered belief in the existence and activity of the devil to be ridiculous. Almost at the same time the scientific world view made its own contribution to dislodge this belief from public consciousness. Finally, this view was taken over by numerous Christian theologians. So Rudolf Bultmann tersely deemed: 'Now that the forces and the laws of nature have been discovered, we can no longer believe in spirits, whether good or evil.'[3] This kind of dismissal of an ancient Christian conviction is certainly much too simplistic to be convincing. On the one hand, the current world view is already different from the time of Bultmann, for the separation of nature and freedom, which was still self-evident for Bultmann, turned out in the meantime to be a fallacy, as we have seen. On the other hand, the experience of evil can not be evaluated from the standpoint of the scientific world view alone. Particularly in instances where humans experience wickedness on a grand scale from their fellow humans, the suspicion may arise, seemingly spontaneously, that the devil may be behind it – for example behind a Hitler, a Stalin, or a Pol Pot. As Christians we should therefore turn again to the Holy Scriptures on this abysmal question.

The Biblical Evidence

For some, the Bible's answer to the question of evil seems simple and clear. Don't the Old and New Testament speak unambiguously of the devil and Satan? Actually these turn up quite often, but also in a confusing way. In the Book of Job Satan appears among the 'sons of God', and he conducts himself with God as though he were an equal. He even induces him to make a wager about Job (Job 1:8–2:10). In other instances it is not clear whether something comes from God or from Satan. Thus in the second Book of Samuel the incitement of David to conduct a census is ascribed to Yahweh (2 Samuel 24:1), while in Chronicles the same incitement is ascribed to Satan (1 Chronicles 21:1). Who is this Satan, who is so close to God and can be confused with him?

It was only in the extracanonical Jewish writings that there first appeared the idea of Satan as an angel, who was thrown out of heaven into hell because of his pride (e.g., Enoch 6:1–7; 10:4–6). However, this idea of the angel's fall was not taken up directly in the Old Testament, and in the New Testament there are only marginal allusions to it (2 Peter 2:4; Jude 6). Are these marginal mentions sufficient to develop a coherent doctrine concerning the devil? Since the controversy over Galileo, and especially since the emergence of modern sciences, which reveal a much longer and more comprehensive history of humanity than the Bible would lead us to presume, we know that we must distinguish between authentic truths of faith and historically conditioned world views in the Holy Scriptures. Is belief in the devil also only a part of an ancient picture of the world?

The devil as *tempter* is the subject in important passages of the New Testament, and he put even Jesus to the test. This fact should warn us from the very start against dissolving him into nothing by merely referring to the world view of that time. The testimonies of the New Testament are certainly quite complex. For instance, the devil appears as an evil power that is not yet defeated and that threatens human beings, yet on the other hand there are clear statements about a victory over him. The enemy not yet defeated is the great tempter and accuser, and he is designated as 'ruler of this world' (John 12:31; 14:30; 16:11), indeed as 'god of this world' (2 Corinthians 4:4). But this overwhelming enemy was driven out through the judgement that takes place on the Cross of Christ (John 12:31) and was deprived of power by the death of Christ (Hebrews 2:14). The contents of both kinds of testimony stand in full agreement with the most central message of the New Testament, which is that Christ on the Cross has accomplished victory over all evil.

That Christ's death on the Cross defeated the devil is indeed the central conviction of the New Testament and the Church. It places us, however, before a difficult exegetical problem. It is striking that nowhere in the Passion narratives is anything said *directly* about a victory over the devil. The Adversary is mentioned as long as he is not overcome and still does his work. It is also clearly said that he is defeated by the crucifixion of Christ. But the Gospels seem never to recount how the defeat is accomplished. Did the whole battle occur in concealment, behind the scenes as it were? This conclusion would be strange, given that the Bible is not a book that intends to conceal, but to reveal. The history of Christianity shows further that the faithful could fall into satanic ways precisely in struggling against Satan. So it would be very helpful and important to know how Christ defeated Satan so that we ourselves would not succumb to evil illusions. And this pastoral and spiritual question is not the only one that is pressing. At least the Gospel of Luke directly requires us to question further, for it ends the narrative of the temptation of Jesus with the following remark: 'When the devil had ended every temptation he departed from him until an opportune time' (*kairou*, 'when the time was ripe', Luke 4:13). The 'opportune time' mentioned here must mean the time of the Cross, when Satan again confronted Jesus. But why doesn't the Gospel report this second, decisive attack if it presented the first and less harmful one in the wilderness?

If we tenaciously pose the question why there is nothing of the devil or Satan in the Passion narratives, we are urged to a hypothesis which must be tested much more precisely in the texts themselves. According to the Gospel of John the devil is 'the father of lies' (John 8:44). And so it must be his essential character to deceive humans not only about the kind and manner of his activity, but *in every-thing*. We must therefore reckon that Satan as undefeated and still able to deceive appears to men differently from the one who is already conquered and has lost his power to deceive. We must interrogate the Gospels as to whether or not the manifestation of the tempter is transformed before our eyes in the process of being overcome, and thus we must put the question to the Passion narratives whether or not they present the defeated Satan in an unexpected way. If we put the question like this, we hit right away upon an answer. The satanic actually plays an important, even central role in the passion narratives of all four Gospels, for Jesus himself is condemned with the accusation that he has spoken satanically. The Synoptic Gospels recount that the high council justified its proceedings against him with the assertion: 'He has uttered blasphemy!' (Matthew 26:65). The Gospel of John makes clear what kind of blasphemy is meant. In it the Jews argue before Pilate, 'We have a law, and by that law he ought to die, because he presented himself as the Son of God' (John 19:7). The same Gospel also makes an explicit connection between this accusation that he presented himself as the Son of God (the charge of blasphemy) and the satanic. In a dispute in which the imminent Passion is foreshadowed, in that the Jews want to stone Jesus, they say: 'We are not stoning you for a good work but for blasphemy. You are only a man, but are making yourself God' (John 10:33). To be a creature and to want to make oneself God is the worst form of blasphemy and the real essence of the satanic. So in the proceedings against Jesus the charge was the most horrendous that could be made. The council accused him of making a claim about himself that was blasphemous in the full sense, i.e., it was a satanic claim.

We have therefore come upon a surprising, yet clear result: the subject of the satanic is not only present in the Passion narratives but it is a crucial element in them, unless we look for the actual figure of the devil. In these accounts we also find both central elements that belong to Satan according to the Jewish tradition, viz. (1) to accuse humans before God (Job 1:6–2:10; Zechariah 3:1) and (2) to be a creature that makes itself God. These two notions admittedly don't fit directly together, for how could a creature accuse humans before God if at the same time it wants to be God itself? Thus the two elements are found in separate places in the Jewish tradition. In the Passion accounts, though, the seemingly contradictory elements converge in a startling way because the will to be as God turns up in the form of accusation against another: Jesus is accused in the name of God (and so before God) that though a creature, he blasphemously claims to be God. But the accusers thereby do nothing other than transfer onto him what he previously disclosed in them (see Mark 3:22–30; 12:1–12; John 8:44). Consequently the satanic appears in the Gospels as a collective religious projection by means of which sinners load onto the sinless one what they do not want to see in their own hearts and so make him to be sin (2 Corinthians 5:21), to be cursed (Galatians 3:13), to be Satan (John 19:7; 10:33) – and in this way make him the scapegoat in a new, complete sense.[4]

The Gospel of John sheds further light on the character of the satanic. In a look back at the entire public work of Jesus it states, 'Although he had performed so many signs in their presence, they (the Jews) did not believe in him' (John 12:37). Then it interprets this negative statement through two Old Testament quotations which address in particular the theme of hardening of hearts, in order finally to conclude with a startling qualification: 'Nevertheless, many, even among the authorities, believed in him; but because of the Pharisees they did not acknowledge it openly, so as not to be expelled from the synagogue' (John 12:42). This qualification shows on the one hand that Jesus, in spite of a lack of external success, reached many people inwardly by his challenging message and fascinating person and could move them to initial belief. On the other hand, it explains exactly why he was nonetheless rejected: Those whose hearts he had won did not dare to commit themselves publicly to him. So in the destiny of Jesus we see that public life has a law completely its own and this was what led to his rejection (John 12:43; see 5:44).

In a world of deception and violence every individual is necessarily threatened and profoundly intimidated. All therefore spontaneously seek good repute, appreciation, and honour in order to feel secure. However, a humanity requiring that each person support and make himself secure through others locks itself in its own prison, and in this situation true faith is impossible (John 5:44). By this reciprocal search for honour and recognition humans balance themselves through one another and thus shield themselves in a self-sufficient way against God. A satanic tendency arises, of which individuals may be largely unaware and in which they become entrapped.

Although Jesus was able to win the hearts of many, his message failed because of the autonomous law of public life and because of the reciprocal striving for honour and recognition. The final tendency of this autonomous law is unveiled in the Passion narratives, for what counted as truth for the public led to the condemnation of Jesus, and indeed he was condemned as a satanic person. If the judgement upon him is fallacious, however, and only reflects what dominated those who condemned him, the final tendency of public life and of the reciprocal struggle for honour is revealed as satanic.[5] So it becomes understandable why the New Testament can identify Satan as 'ruler of this world' (John 12:31) and as 'god of this world' (2 Corinthians 4:4).[6]

As long as Satan is not overcome he can make himself very much like the image of God (one of the 'sons of God'). He manifests himself for the time being as a distinct figure, which apparently enters our world from a transcendent world and tries here to seduce human beings to do evil. In this way he also faced Jesus at the beginning of his public ministry and confronted him with the whole force of the collective expectations of this world. In this first confrontation, earthly wishes along the lines of Old Testament notions crystallized for Jesus into a seductive form (Matthew 4:1–11). Soon after that, however, Jesus saw Satan, who previously belonged to the world of the sacred (see Job), fall like lightning from heaven (Luke 10:18). From then on it may have become quite clear for Jesus that the actual temptation arises from human beings. Even Peter did not understand the difference between 'what God wants' and 'what humans want' (Matthew 16:23), so Jesus had to rebuff his chosen disciple as 'Satan'.

But the true extent of this unmasking of the satanic remained hidden for the moment. Particularly for the opponents of Jesus Satan remained (unnoticed by them) in heaven, i.e., in their image of God. They could thus raise the claim to act in God's name and at the same time reject the one God actually sent as a blasphemer. However, since Jesus had long since seen through the actual tempter, this judgement could no longer shake him inwardly in any way. He did not need to react with an aggressive counter-accusation, but was able to be silent, pray for his enemies, and give everything over to the true judgement of his heavenly Father. The Father justified him by the resurrection. Easter therefore shows how the accusation falls back on the accusers. The very one cast out as Satan was acknowledged by God as the true Son (against the presumed 'son of God'), was made to be the author of eternal life, and installed as the centre of the new people of God: 'The stone the builders rejected has become the cornerstone' (Mark 12:10).[7] Thus the defeat of Satan turns out to be the centre of a dramatically understood doctrine of redemption.

Four Great Themes of the Image of Satan

In our investigation two great themes which are traditionally connected to the devil were seamlessly conjoined: making accusations before God[8] and self-deification, thereby shedding new light on both themes. From both perspectives the satanic appears as the collective dimension of evil, as the tendency of a humanity which locks itself up and projects the hidden evil onto others. With this interpretation self-deification becomes more understandable. It does not consist in the insane determination of a creature to come out openly and with raised fist against God. How could this be, since he or she is dependent on God in everything and in every way? Rather, self-deification originates, in fact in an instinctive mechanism of reciprocal imitation, of anxiety and the quest for honour, by which human beings lock themselves into their world, which drifts towards hell. Humans are agents in a process in which they simultaneously become victims. The collective tendency in which they are caught is usually not transparent to them, and they own up even less to the mutual dependency. So from this comes the propensity to accuse others and to unload their evil onto a third party.

Our interpretation is supported by the fact that in its light we may conjoin two more themes of the satanic to the two already mentioned: hardening the heart and being possessed. The theme of hardening is addressed in the Gospel of John, as already noted. There it explains why

Jesus was, in spite of the faith of many, rejected. In this regard Isaiah 6:9–10 is quoted: 'He blinded their eyes and hardened their heart, so that they might not see with their eyes and understand with their heart and be converted, so that I could heal them' (John 12:40). In the Book of Isaiah it seems that God is the one who hardens the heart. But the wording of the quotation in John corresponds neither to the Masoretic text nor to the Septuagint nor to the Targum. Schnackenburg thus rightly concludes from his analysis 'that the form of the quotation derives from no-one but the evangelist'.[9] Because of this changing of the text the question arises as to what the Gospel writer wanted to say and who in his view is the hardener of the heart ('he' in the text) and who the healer is ('I' in the text). Schnackenburg holds that by 'he' and 'I' the Evangelist means God and Christ. God hardens, so Christ may not heal. This interpretation would raise a serious theological problem, for in this case God would be the direct author of morally evil deeds. Yet, in the context of our previous analysis Schnackenburg's interpretation is hardly tenable. Since it is very clearly indicated in John 12:42–43 that the hardening has effect by means of the mechanism of reciprocal fear of certain human authorities and since our previous analysis shows that this mechanism is identical with Satan, another interpretation is suggested. This is that the fear of other humans, or Satan, in other terms, is the agent that hardens the heart and Christ is the healer. This interpretation is in accord with the central theme of the Christian message.[10]

We can clarify the theme of possession in similar fashion. As collective projections and accusations are extremely powerful, they affect their victims deeply from within. The possessed are those who submit to a collective accusation in the name of an otherworldly power, who experience a total inward breakdown, and who completely internalize the evil judgement that others make about them.[11] Victims such as these no longer exercise their own judgement and have no will of their own, for the collective projection in which they believe controls them as an alien will and commands them what to do. This projection is the work of many, so for the possessed the number of demons is often legion (Mark 5:1–20).[12]

Finally we would connect the four themes with a theology of history. Collective projections certainly play a preeminent role in the life of peoples and in human history. L. Poliakov has shown in his great classical work on anti-Semitism[13] how the respective societies continually oppressed the Jews as scapegoats. Poliakov, however, did not stop with this insightful observation. In a later, two-volume work, which refers to the diabolic in the title,[14] he offered a critical addendum by demonstrating that not only the Jews, but also other groups were forced to assume the role of the enemy or scapegoat. Above all he shows that in the great European revolutions – the English, French, and Russian – images of the enemy were of critical significance for their success. In all three of these, acting in unity was only made possible by conspiracy theories and false images of enemies. These great revolutions, in which many see the milestones of the modern history of freedom, turn out to be classic examples of the scapegoat mechanism or the 'causalité diabolique'.[15]

The Meaning of the Serpent and the Apocalyptic Animals

The unmasking of the figure of Satan as a collective mechanism leads us back to the question of original sin. Traditional theology interpreted the serpent in paradise as the devil. In the third chapter we saw, however, that the entire paradise narrative should be interpreted anew in light of the New Testament. The theme of the serpent has been omitted so far, but now we will make up for that. An initial answer comes quickly to mind. Already in the first chapter, an interpretation was suggested to us through an internal analysis of the garden story: the serpent is a symbol of that mimesis which becomes enslaved to immediate desire through restrictive imitation. However, this mimesis is largely identical with the reciprocal quest for honour and the corresponding collective projections. Accordingly, the serpent would indeed be a symbol for the devil, if we mean by that the mechanisms of collective evil rather than an otherworldly figure. Christ has fundamentally unmasked and defeated these mechanisms on the Cross and so trampled down the head of the serpent (see Genesis 3:15).

With this answer, however, a further question asserts itself: why did an animal become the symbol for restrictive imitation, the mutual search for approval, and the collective mechanisms of evil? In *Deceit, Desire, and the Novel* Girard analyses how passionate desire is described in modern literary works. He comes to a conclusion that could be surprising at first. An idol has a more seductive effect the more unapproachable it is, and it is all the more unapproachable the closer it comes to the automatic reaction of instincts, even to a lifeless, mechanical character. The absurd project of self-deification tends therefore to move towards animal life and even ends by seeking the divine in what is lifeless.[16] This astute observation readily clarifies why so many gods were represented as animals over and over again in archaic religions and why lifeless idols can awaken such great fascination. The same observation makes intelligible why the serpent was the actual seducer for the biblical narrator. Its creeping nature affects humans as particularly unapproachable, even frightening. And both animals in the Apocalypse of John are similarly frightening and fascinating. They allure human desire into wonderment, even to worship.

In the context of the primal scene, as we sketched it out of the background of the theory of evolution in the third chapter, and in light of Girard's observation, we can determine a still larger meaning for symbols from the animal world. If the first humans were summoned to a yet unknown future as they emerged from the animal world, then this new experience of moving beyond previous limitations must have awakened in them an inner uncertainty. In this situation the fascinating security of instinct and the unapproachable character of their animal past could spontaneously congeal into an image that easily settled over the newly sensed remoteness of the unknown future and thus became a seductive phantasm. In a consciousness still scarcely reflective the new presentiment of the future and the divine could easily, almost unawares, be suppressed by another powerful pull, the undertow of the past.

The logic of desire as described by Girard can certainly also shed an illuminating light on our modern world. Idols of the public that are able to put themselves into states of ecstasy, which are ruled only by the certainty of their instinctual drives, have an especially fascinating effect and attract great masses of people. But the logic of desire is not restricted to mass phenomena. It may even influence scientific research, zeroing in particularly on the realm of the lifeless. Why are there so many scientists who think they are especially bold, insightful, and enlightened, when they render man as far as possible into a mechanical being? Why do such authors in scientific circles win such high recognition? There must be a fascination that comes from the realm of the lifeless and the mechanical. In the Revelation of John the greatest success of the second beast comes in fact from its ability to bestow the breath of life on a dead image (Revelation 13:15). But what life does this mean? Isn't it the subtlest perversion that science might be able to create a mechanical form of life?

F. Tippler in his *Physics of Immortality* presents a physics in which he tries to explain God and the resurrection of the dead by physical formulas. He delineates a vision of a life that extends gradually in a digital fashion from our planet into the whole cosmos. Is this life anything more than the most complex, mechanistic information? In Girard's analysis of the logic of desire the imitator imitates his model and the model his imitator, until both appear indistinguishable from an observer's point of view. According to this logic, the living yearns for the lifeless and the lifeless for the living, until both are indistinguishable to everyday eyes.

Is Satan Only a Collective Mechanism – or Something More?

Our brief investigation of Satan has not been based on any sort of modern and fashionable assumptions. We intended only to follow the text of the New Testament, and we have been fully engaged with those questions which the text itself poses. What significance can we now assign to our results? It is indisputable that the New Testament uncovers the collective dimension of evil and brings it clearly into connection with the theme of the satanic. Since projection belongs to the basic character of Satan, it is understandable how difficult he is to overcome. What we project, we see only in others and not in ourselves. Thus the persecutors of witches discovered the devil only in their victims, and they never became aware that their own system of persecution was satanic.

However, does the collective projection arising out of a reciprocal quest for honour expose the entire reality of Satan? This question is hard to answer because evil is a mystery for which we never quite find the clue, so we must finally speak of it in images. If we attend to the Passion narratives we find in fact no allusions to a broader dimension of Satan. But as long as we have not experienced the abysmal and deadly power of collective accusations in the most profound way, we must speak metaphorically of Satan so as not to trivialize evil. And as long as we remain sinners without having overcome evil, it may appear to us again and again as a figure in its own right. Therefore the New Testament writings, even after Easter, speak of the devil as a distinct figure. This post-Easter language of Satan therefore presents no objection to our interpretation.

The biblical authors, in speaking of the devil, were aware of the metaphorical character of their statements. This is made clear in an example from the Revelation of John. In Revelation 12:7–9 the battle of Michael and his angels against the dragon and his followers is described, initially by means of very apocalyptic images. Then the dragon is identified as Satan, who is defeated in heaven and with his adherents cast to the earth. Immediately after their downfall, however, a loud voice sounds which reports the event once again but with completely different words. This voice first of all proclaims the victory, and at the same time lays bare what Satan did in heaven before his fall: 'Now salvation and power ... has come ..., for the accuser of our brothers is thrown down, who accused them day and night before our God' (Revelation 12:10). Satan was the great accuser. Immediately after the announcement of victory the voice proclaims further who defeated this accuser: 'They conquered him by the blood of the Lamb and the word of their testimony; love for life did not deter them from death' (Revelation 12:11). The victors over Satan are clearly the Christian martyrs. What is ascribed to Michael and his angels in heaven by the metaphorical language, is interpreted as the victory of the martyrs thanks to the blood of Christ by the voice speaking immediately after this. The victory in heaven is thus the victory in the community of the believers in Christ. On earth, however, i.e., in the collective mechanisms of human society, Satan continues to rage as reciprocal accusation.

The truth which the New Testament and especially the Passion narratives reveal about Satan demands a total conversion and still is before us. As long as the evil in our heart is not fully overcome it must appear, again and again, as a distinct figure. The New Testament writings therefore always speak of it in a double form: as a distinct figure and as a collective power located in humanity. The task of conversion and victory over the devil is to uncover how much we ourselves are entrenched in the accusatory powers. To the extent that we overcome them, the figure of Satan will disappear before our eyes. But even then, does it completely disappear?

Evil is a mystery whose clue we never completely perceive because we ourselves remain attached to it. So in the end, we must always speak of it in metaphors; therefore it is problematic to assert categorically that the devil is merely (!) a collective projection. For the Old and New Testaments it is self-evident that humans are not the only spiritual creatures. In the Scriptures angels appear almost everywhere, and in this context the supposition that some of them – similar to humans – have fallen is rather suggestive. Christian theology has understood angels as pure spirits that are also creatures. Such notions are certainly difficult in contemporary metaphysics, for a relation to matter seems to belong to every creature.[17] For this reason K. Rahner seeks in his reflections on angels to show first of all, by means of general considerations concerning revelation, that today one must leave the question open as to whether acceptance of angels and demons belongs to the binding deposit of faith.[18] Under the presupposition that there are actually such beings he opposes the idea of angels as pure spirits:

> In the first place, we may be allowed to register a protest against the generally accepted view in angelology and demonology that these created 'spirits' must be seen as 'pure' spirits without necessarily possessing an essential relationship to matter. These beings may be 'pure' spirits insofar as they neither are merely material realities nor possess that materiality which belongs to man in virtue of his bodily nature. But to go beyond this in describing the angels and demons as 'pure' spirits may be Neoplatonic philosophy; it is neither the Church's teaching as binding in faith nor logically implied in the fact that these beings have no body in form that we ourselves know as human.[19]

Rahner tries then to conceive of angels as cosmic actualizations of essences (entelechies) or subjective minds whose task is to guide and to organize[20] certain greater realms of the cosmos – for example, the evolution of life on earth or certain areas of life (plants and animals), but also 'periods of the history of mankind' or 'histories of individual nations'.[21] In the context of an evolutionary world view he holds it conceivable, even probable, that the development of the world across qualitative leaps not only produced human beings but also 'has already reached those subjectivities with a greater material regionality which we call angels'.[22] Demons would then be the sort of essences or entelechies that have made a negative resolve against God and so exercise a negative influence over that part of the material world[23] to which they are assigned.

Besides conceiving of this kind of extra-terrestrial subjective minds and devils, there is still another possibility. In view of contemporary knowledge that billions of stars already belong to our Milky Way and that our galaxy is only one in a billion, we must ask whether there could be human-like beings on other planets.[24] Astronomy has recently demonstrated for the first time that there are actually other planets outside our solar system. If this holds true, then, because of the uniformity of natural laws in the universe, we must immediately reckon with an innumerable abundance of such planets. Researchers have accounted further for chemical combinations in the cosmos which come close to organic combinations, and on Mars there even seems to have been a primitive form of life. These strands of evidence suggest that the conditions for life could be present in many places.

If there should in fact be other human-like rational beings elsewhere in the cosmos, they – like us – must face the choice between good and evil. Will some of these 'humanities' decide only for the good or have they already decided? Will others fall almost entirely into evil? Is there also some kind of redemption for other fallen humanities? Many questions come to mind for which we scarcely have the beginning of an answer at present. But if there should be other such humankinds, then we have to assume – on account of the unity of creation – that their good and bad deeds also exercise a certain influence on us, even if it is impossible for us to determine exactly the kind of effect they have. However, this influence may be compared to what one traditionally called angels or devils.

Our brief thoughts show that the language of angels and devils raises many questions, questions that must be seriously posed even if this results in leaving just as many questions open. In spite of this, however, possibilities emerge which suggest how we might speak of an extra-terrestrial devil in a new way. To be sure, the time may not yet be ripe for clear answers in this realm. Certainly, many people have experiences which strongly suggest dimensions of creaturely reality that transcend our quotidian experience. Yet how these experiences should be precisely construed must remain open for the time being.

It should be clear, however, that a position basically denying the existence of angels and demons hardly arises from clear insight, but rather reflects a rationalistic prejudice. Both our general reflections on the existence of angels along the lines of Rahner's thought and our biblical deconstruction of the devil make clear that revolting devils and puckish demons clearly belong to mythology. Evil is always to be sought first and foremost in human hearts and in human relations. This certainly does not exclude that human decisions are made in an environment that may be positively or negatively influenced by other 'subjective minds' by means of the material world.

The 'Battle' against Evil

Even if we do not categorically claim that the interpretation of Satan as a collective projection exhausts the whole reality of evil, it is nonetheless important because it furnishes clues as to how the 'evil enemy' is to be fought. Since projections easily awaken counter-projections, they are never overcome through direct attacks but are even reinforced that way. Evil cannot be fought frontally, but can only be overcome by the slow development of a true vision of reality. This has to occur differently in different spheres of human life.

Collective projections are very powerful in the form of inherited enmities between entire peoples, which also reflect very clearly mankind's burden of original sin. Such inherited forms of evil are so powerful that Christian men and women must often be included in those who do not recognize them; they are the reason why so many wars, with corresponding self-righteousness, occurred even among Christian peoples. For religious people it is often especially hard to see through national prejudices because, as history shows, there were many kinds of commingling between religion and nationalism, and this is still true today. To combat the devil in this area of life and to clear away the inheritance of evil involves above all talking to those neighbours whom we have condemned by our own nationalistic feeling and labelled as inhuman or demonic. For dialogues such as these the words of Jesus should show the way: 'Judge not, that you be not judged! For as you judge, so shall you be judged, and the measure you give will be the measure you get. Why do you see the speck in your brother's eye and do not notice the log that is in your own?' (Matthew 7:1–3). Whoever holds another people to be worse than his own judges others and thereby judges himself, for he overlooks the log that is in his own eye. This sort of restraint in judging, however, goes against our spontaneous tendency. To renounce the condemnation of others requires therefore a constant spiritual process that includes an ever deeper recognition of our own sinfulness. But the growing recognition of the evil in our own heart would only differ from self-torment, if our gaze at evil simultaneously included the question of inherited evil. Only a doctrine of original sin that is deeply steeped in the wisdom of lived experience can enable us to see evil with clarity and preserve us from condemning others and ourselves even more.

There are also collective projections in other spheres, especially between adherents of different religions. These are at least as stubborn and just as difficult to overcome as national prejudices. It holds true especially for the religions of revelation because they live out of the conviction that they are based not on human experience, but directly on the word of God. The believers of these religions are thus spontaneously tempted to categorize everything they find baffling or disturbing in other religions as impious or satanic. Precisely for this reason Jesus was condemned as a blasphemer, and for similar reasons there have been many evil events in Christian history (persecution of Jews, crusades, religious wars, etc.). The task of clearing away condemnatory projections like these without diluting one's own convictions and falling into a rootless relativism is difficult. Yet a lapse into relativism only awakens new fundamentalisms with their corresponding projections. A first step on the way to this task is to gain the insight that long before Abraham, in whom the special acts of God began according to all three great religions of revelation, divine providence guided humanity. In light of the theory of evolution and the view of the cosmos, as contemporary science portrays it, God's ways in the world prove to be far more complex and long-range. We can therefore never know what plans divine providence pursues with the adherents of foreign religions, and in view of the massive size and complexity of the creation this question also loses much of its troubling significance.

The massive changes that the modern world view has brought with it show further that from today's viewpoint one can only regard the Holy Scriptures as books of revelation in all honesty, if one distinguishes in them between the word of revelation and the world view in whose frame of reference the word was received. This distinction is not an incipient relativism but a clear sign that we are ready to ever again distinguish the true God from idolatrous images. As Girard shows, such idolatrous images arise spontaneously from the collective mechanism of projection. The gradual overcoming of these projections, or of Satan, and the task of distinguishing between world view and the true God belong together. Precisely this process of distinguishing, however, should make us careful about evaluating people in other religions. Their faith intentions can be more true and more profound than we are able to assume from their formulations in language.

And conversely, we must consider that our formulations too are problematic for others; indeed, they may come across as offensive and idolatrous. That form of the satanic which consists in spontaneously demonizing adherents of other religions is most readily overcome if we use the differences between the religions to ask ourselves constantly whether we serve the true God or have covertly fallen into some sort of idolatry. What can easily occasion the demonizing of others can also be used in the other direction. As soon as we see through the originally sinful tendency to create idols, the differences among the religions can become an especially effective means of purifying our own faith ever anew.

As a final point I would mention something that makes it clear why Satan is so difficult to defeat. Everyone easily understands that collective projections are bad to the extent that they burden others with false judgements. However, we are likely to overlook that such projections also have a positive effect for our own group or our own people – at least for the short term. Images of the enemy create external unity and weld our own group together. They are thus instinctively sought and spontaneously believed. The task of overcoming projections is therefore far more than a theoretical one. The challenge is to find new and much more difficult practical ways to create unity without scapegoating. Modern psychology and sociology have long pointed to the problem of projections, yet they have scarcely changed anything. Criticizing collective projections amounts to little or nothing as long as we are unable to achieve the unity among human beings necessary for human life by other means. Satan, or the scapegoat mechanism with its projections, is thus the 'ruler of this world' because he spontaneously brings about this unity, although in a deceptive fashion and at the expense of others. To gain victory over him means to create unity both by owning up to our failings, especially those of which we are not aware (original sin), and by practising forgiveness ever anew.

Notes

1 C.f. Boberski, *Das Engelwerk*; Lindsey, *The Late Great Planet Earth*; Stocker, *Prophezeiungen über bevorstehende Ereignissse*.

2 C.f. U.P. Lange, 'Die dreifache, sich steigernde Offensive Satans, des "Fürsten dieser Welt", gegen die Kirche', in *Una Voce Korrespondenz* 15 (1985), 84–87. For an overview: J. Niewiadomski, 'Wohl tobet um die Mauern ... ', in *Die Verdrängte Freiheit*, 156–180.

3 Bultmann, *Kerygma and Myth*, 1–44, here 4.

4 The question of Satan is seamlessly connected to that of hell. C.f. Schwager, *Jesus in the Drama of Salvation*, 63–69, 83–93, 159–169.

5 Girard arrives at this result in another way, namely through the analysis of the New Testament theme of 'skandalon'. C.f. Girard, *Things Hidden*, 416–431.

6 According to the New Testament, Satan is both the principle of disorder (tempter) and the principle of order (ruler of this world). This seeming contradiction is solved, when Satan is identified with mimetic desire and the scapegoat mechanism. C.f. Girard, *Quand ces choses commenceront*, 76f.

7 In saying this, Jesus concludes the parable of the evil vinedressers in which the subject is also the satanic: the vinedressers kill the son because they want to seize the inheritance of the Lord (the heavenly Father) for themselves.

8 Girard sees in the contrast between Satan, the accuser, and the Paraclete, the comforter and defender of victims, a central thread of the Gospels and a succinct summary of his own thinking. C.f. Girard, *The Scapegoat*, 205–212.

9 Schnackenburg, *The Gospel According to St John* (vol. 2), 415.

10 The interpretation that Satan is the one who hardens was the opinion of Cyril of Alexandria, 'Fragment zu Joh 12:40' (*PG* 74, 96f); Blank, *Crisis*, 304f.

11 C.f. Oughourlian, *The Puppet of Desire*; Kufulu Mandunu, *Das 'Kindoki' im Licht der Sündenbocktheologie*.

12 C.f. Girard, *The Scapegoat*, 165–183.

13 Poliakov, *The History of Anti-Semitism* (4 vols.).

14 Poliakov, *La causalité diabolique*.

15 The view of Poliakov is easily confirmed and extended in further works. C.f. Ch. Meier, *Die Entstehung des Politischen bei den Griechen*; Jeismann, *Das Vaterland der Feinde*; Schmitt, *Der Begriff des Politischen*; Sobrino, *Sterben muss, wer an Götzen rührt*.

16 'The Other is more fascinating the less accessible he is; and the more despiritualized he is, the more he tends toward an instinctive automatism, the more inaccessible he is. And the absurd project of self-divinization ends up by going beyond the animal to the automatic and even the mechanical. The individual becomes increasingly bewildered and unbalanced by a desire which nothing can satisfy and finally seeks the divine essence in that which radically denies his own existence: the inanimate.' Girard, *Deceit, Desire, and the Novel*, 286.

17 C.f. Rahner, *Geist in Welt*.

18 Rahner, 'On Angels', in idem, *Theological Investigations* 19, 235–274, especially 240–252.

19 Ibid., 253–254.

20 'Even a human reality which itself represents a corporeally limited system of matter and subjectivity can be conceived as integrated into such a higher system, if and insofar as this corporality itself has a potentiality for a higher and more comprehensive order. If two subjectivities are thus understood as graded principles of unity and order, with one above the other, then, of course, such a gradation and sub- and super-ordination is originally present in connection with this organizing function in regard to matter as such only insofar as these two principles extend to a smaller ('body') or greater material area ('angelic region') but not (as is obvious) insofar as both principles as intellectual subjects of freedom have an infinite openness to being as a whole and to God.' Ibid., 264.

21 Ibid., 270.

22 Ibid., 266.

23 'At the same time it should not be forgotten that the meaning and function of such principles of unity and order are not intended properly and primarily to influence man's freedom, but to establish a unity and order (within a particular region) in the material world, although they can take the form of a temptation for man, if and insofar as such orders may in their principles imply a rejection of God's gracious self-communication, carrying in themselves a tendency to be closed up, to become absolute.' Ibid., 271–272.

24 Rahner explicitly brackets this question on the basis that such beings, if there be any, are not drawn existentially into our human environment (ibid., 262–263). Many films whose theme is extraterrestrial beings similar to humans seem to show however that this has become a vital question today and perhaps points to a deeper existential dimension.

A Political Epilogue

The problem of original sin and the closely related question of the devil and collective evil have led us to the theme of the battle against evil. These questions have political implications, which were also hinted at earlier in connection with genetic technology. These implications should now, in conclusion, be highlighted somewhat more clearly. This is also quite urgent because for decades a comprehensive interpretation of politics and a political theology has existed in which the doctrine of original sin plays an important role. I have in mind the work of Carl Schmitt, who because of his connection to National Socialism was unable to have an academic role in the post-war period. Nonetheless, his influence has continued to be felt and he has 'again achieved a certain importance in the contemporary (not only German) scene', as J.B. Metz states.[1]

Schmitt has affected the realm of political thought particularly through his distinction between friend and enemy, and it is just this distinction that for decades has so troubled his critics. On the one hand one presumes that this definition of the political produces a closeness to National Socialism, while on the other hand it is hard to deny that this addresses something essential in the political history of humankind, as brief references can easily show.

The most profound insight into politics and democracy among the Greeks, as Ch. Meier demonstrates,[2] is found not in the work of Aristotle, as is usually assumed, but in Aeschylus. In the *Eumenides* the tragedian shows how the violent system of blood revenge is overcome by a new system of justice, a new city-state order. From the violent Erinnyes, the goddesses of vengeance, the gentle and beneficial Eumenides emerge. But this fundamental change, which includes the transition to free citizenship, occurs only as violence is reallocated: 'So here we have friendship within the city, and united hostility directed outside it. Mutual murder is to be replaced by mutual giving of joy. Enmity is no longer to be directed inward, but outward, in a spirit of solidarity. There is to be a new, polis-oriented distinction between friend and ... [enemy], a shift in the friend-...[enemy] relationship. In this way the polis will attain unity.'[3]

L. Poliakov, whom we encountered already in connection with the question of collective projections, speaks from a quite different area of research in coming to the same conclusion. In his work *La causalité diabolique* he showed that images of the enemy played a decisive role in the great European revolutions, the English, the French, and the Russian. That is, in all three cases the unity of action among the revolutionaries was made possible only through conspiracy theories and false images of the enemy.[4] The modern history of freedom[5] thus substantiates how significant the friend-enemy distinction is in the political realm.[6]

After the defeat of National Socialism in World War II many believed initially that only the 'evil' communists still bore responsibility that there was no universal peace. The cessation of this worldwide friend-enemy polarization now indicates, however, that having a common enemy suppressed a lot of inner conflicts. Thus U. Beck, who can surely not be suspected of sympathy with totalitarian thought, states:

> In all democracies so far there have been two kinds of authority. One originates from the people, the other from the enemy. Images of the enemy integrate. Images

of the enemy empower. Images of the enemy have the highest priority for conflict. They allow the overriding and subordination of all other social conflicts. They represent the an alternative source of energy, so to speak, for consensus, which is becoming scarce, as modernity advances.[7]

What Beck states so soberly, populist leaders and demagogues have always known and deployed for their political goals.

With insights like these Schmitt supports his central thesis, and he relates it to a political anthropology according to which 'all genuine political theories presuppose man to be evil, i.e., by no means an unproblematic but a dangerous and dynamic being'.[8] Schmitt holds that this anthropology stands in clear connection with the doctrine of original sin: 'The fundamental theological dogma of the evilness of the world and man leads, just as does the distinction of friend and enemy, to categorization of men and makes impossible the undifferentiated optimism of a universal conception of man.'[9] Schmitt appears convinced that no Christian theology can bypass this view of the world: 'A Theologian ceases to be a theologian when he no longer considers man to be sinful or in need of redemption and no longer distinguishes between those redeemed and those not redeemed, between the chosen and the nonchosen. The moralists presupposes a freedom of choice between good and evil.'[10] In a later work, *Politische Theologie II*, Schmitt even attempted to base his friend-enemy distinction on the doctrine of the Trinity.[11]

For every Christian theology that wants to avoid the perception of being too close to National Socialism, Schmitt's position is challenging and for many even distressing. This political thinker has long been passed over in near-silence, and today some try to distance themselves completely from his anthropology and his basic political principle without delving into them at all.[12] But scarcely anything is gained in this way, for the great influence of Schmitt may just lie in the fact that his friend-enemy relation bears an indisputable connection to the real history of humanity, which lends to his theory a great analytical power. Moreover, the doctrine of the universality of sin is widely anchored in the biblical writings and church tradition. Not only that, original sin, as we have seen, is irreplaceable if one would both hold on to the concern for radical freedom and come to terms with the concrete facts of human life and history.

So a debate with Schmitt is imposed on us, and for some years Wolfgang Palaver in particular has undertaken it, in a number of new essays.[13] He is able to show that Schmitt's political thinking has a (pagan) mythical background and represents an attempt to interpret Christian theology against this background and analyse it for the sake of his political thought. For coming to terms with his political theology one should neither globally reject nor globally follow it. This requires a constant clear-sighted distinction. Palaver shows that in this respect Girard's thought, in which the friend-enemy distinction likewise plays a significant role, is particularly helpful.

Girard goes both back behind Schmitt and beyond him. The friend-enemy relation presupposes political entities that are already constituted. Girard's theory moreover explains how a general situation of crisis leads, by the discharge of collective aggressions against an accidental victim (the scapegoat mechanism), to the separation of internal and external, profane and sacred, familiar and dangerous. Only against this background, and only after the stabilization of political entities, can the friend-enemy relation in Schmitt's sense play a role. Girard differs further from Schmitt in that he does not appeal to biblical passages to legitimize and immortalize the elements actually playing such a great role in politics. He maintains that the Jewish-Christian revelation has just the contrary basic impulse: it aims at overcoming the friend-enemy relation through nonviolence and love of enemy.[14] There is therefore not only the old political theology of Schmitt and the more recent one associated with the name of Metz, but a third version inspired by Girard. The latter shares with Schmitt the view that the friend-enemy distinction in fact plays a great role in political history and that the doctrine of original sin is to be taken seriously. With the more recent political theology it shares the conviction that the Christian message has to overcome the friend-enemy relation as far as possible. For that, good will and 'anamnetic reason' (Metz) alone are not enough. To the contrary, in the history of humanity, and above all in the history of the Christian message, there appears a dramatic struggle between contending powers, a struggle which in modern times has not abated but has even increased in somewhat more subtle forms. In view of this dramatic struggle we need, on the one hand, a cool clear-sightedness, which does not close its eyes before whatever is hostile and try to argue it away; on the other hand, faith in a real redemption is necessary, so that in the long run negative mechanisms will not be taken for natural occurrences which would be totally unchangeable.

Girard's perspective on political theology is in accord with Schmitt's in that a theologian in fact ceases to be a Christian theologian 'if he no longer holds that humans are sinful or in need of redemption'. But this in no way means – against Schmitt – that we have to distinguish 'between those redeemed and those not redeemed, between the chosen and the nonchosen'.[15] Augustine's doctrine of predestination by no means follows with internal logical consistency from his doctrine of original sin. The former is certainly very problematic and is best held at bay from the political realm, as Augustine himself saw. The doctrine of the universality of sin, however, is no threat to democracy, as Metz seems to think. The contrary is more likely the case. The doctrine of original sin demands self-criticism and thus readiness to compromise, which is so decisive for any democracy. Horkheimer and Luhmann explicitly recognized this, as indicated in the introduction. At the present time democracy is in fact being swamped by a world of visual media, with arguments drowned out by a flood of images. It is endangered by economic forces, which substitute the influence of money for actual discussion.

In light of the world-spanning media and economic forces, counter-institutions are necessary that are likewise world spanning and are based neither on money nor the fashions of the media world. The Church as such a counter-institution is of course often helpless and powerless; yet it keeps fundamental alternatives open and so, in spite of problems in its own ranks, resists the tendency to gradually substitute marketing strategies for democracy, which in subtle ways revert completely to the friend-enemy distinction. The doctrine of original sin does not create our political problems, but it certainly circumscribes the greatness of the task. It enables us to judge which proposed solutions are realistic, and thus guards us against counterproductive and bitter consequences of utopian experiments while making clear that only a faith that can move mountains will be able to bring about genuine improvements in history.

Notes

1 Metz, 'Monotheismus und Demokratie', 49; see also this statement: 'Schmitt is, for example, extolled in the discourse of the New Right as 'the most recent classical thinker of political thought', documented by sometime extreme Maoists as an instructive dialogue partner and by liberals and social democrats remembered as a founding father of the [German]constitution ...' Rainer, 'C. Schmitt und J.B. Metz in fremder Nähe?', 83; Laak, 'Gespräche in der Sicherheit des Schweigens'; Habermas, *Die Normalität*, 112–122.

2 Meier, *The Greek Discovery of the Political*.

3 Ibid., 116. Translator's note: Translation corrected, because Schmitt's usage of *Feind* is better rendered enemy – and not foe – in English. Cf. Translator's note in Schmitt, *The Concept of the Political*, 26.

4 H. Arendt seeks to modify this view by emphasizing the difference between the American and the French revolution. The latter attempted to construct the new state through violence, whereas the former was grounded in a communicative power (*The Human Condition*, 228–229). Certainly there are clear differences between the two revolutions. However, Arendt overlooks that for the Americans violence was only more diffuse (England as enemy – chronic battle against Indians and among themselves – war against Mexico). Above all, however, Arendt herself doesn't fail to speak, with Jefferson, of slavery as the 'primordial crime upon which the

fabric of American society rested'. (*On Revolution*, 71.) Yet she draws no further consequences from this insight. C.f. Palaver, 'Foundational violence and Hannah Arendt's Political Philosophy'.

5   That the friend-enemy relation is particularly central for totalitarian regimes is a long recognized result of research. C.f. *Wege der Totalitarianismus-Forschung*, ed. V. Seidel.

6   C.f. also Gay, *Kult der Gewalt*.

7   Beck, *Der feindlose Staat*, 65.

8   Schmitt, *The Concept of the Political*, 61.

9   Ibid., 65. 'What the denial or original sin means socially and from the viewpoint of individual psychology has been shown by Ernst Troeltsch in his *Soziallehren der christlichen Kirchen und Gruppen* and Seillière (in many publications about romanticism and romantics) in the examples of numerous sects, heretics, romantics, and anarchists.' Ibid, 64.

10   Ibid., 64.

11   Schmitt, *Politische Theologie* II, 116–123.

12   'While the new political theology takes its point of departure from the universality of suffering, without exposing itself to the myth of the freedom from suffering, Schmitt's political theology bases itself on the universality of sin, particularly original sin. Schmitt's skepticism concerning the capability of man to achieve a democratic self-government is rooted in this universality, and his basic political principle of the friend-enemy constellation also stems from it.' Metz, *Monotheismus und Demokratie*, 49.

13   Palaver's writings on Schmitt: 'A Girardian Reading of Schmitt's Political Theology'; 'Schmitt's Critique of Liberalism'; 'Die politische Theologie des Grossinquisitors'; 'Das Arkanum in der Politik'; 'Ein doppelte Lektüre der "Politischen Theologie" Carl Schmitts'; 'Carl Schmitt on Nomos and Space'; *Die mythischen Quellen des Politischen*.

14   The friend-enemy relation is biblically connected to the theme of the devil. By analysing the turning around of the diffuse, mutual tendency to acts of aggression into the violence of all against one (scapegoat mechanism), Girard can explain why the devil appears in Scripture both as *diabolos*, the principle of confusion and disorder, and as Satan, the principle of (totalitarian) order (ruler of the world). C.f. Girard, *The Scapegoat*, 184–197.

15   Schmitt, *The Concept of the Political*, 64.

Works Cited

Aggression: Naturwissenschaftliche und kulturwissenschaftliche Perspektiven der Aggressionsforschung, ed. Hilke, et al. Bern 1982.

Anfänge der Christologie (Festschrift. F. Hahn), ed. C. Breytenbach, et al. Göttingen 1991.

Anselm von Canterbury, *Cur deus homo*. Lateinisch und Deutsch. Besorgt von F. Schmitt. Darmstadt 1956.

The Apostolic Fathers with Justin Martyr and Irenaeus. Chronologically Arranged, with Notes by A. Cleveland Coxe. Peabody (Massachusetss): Hendrickson Publishers 21995, 548.

Arendt, H., *Fragwürdige Traditionsbestände im politischen Denken der Gegenwart: Vier Essays*. Frankfurt a. M. 1957.

Arendt, H., *On Revolution*. New York: Viking Press, 1965.

Arendt, H., *The Human Condition*. Chicago: The University of Chicago Press, 1958.

Balthasar, H. U. von, *Cosmic Liturgy: The Universe According to Maximus Confessor*. Tr. B. Daley. San Francisco: Ignatius Press, 2003.

Balthasar, H. U. von. Theodramatik (4 Bde). Einsiedeln 1973–1983. [English Edition: *Theo-drama: Theological Dramatic Theory*, Vol.3: The Dramatis Personae: The Person in Christ. San Francisco: Ignatius, 1992.]

Bandera, C. *The Sacred Game: The Role of the Sacred in the Genesis of Modern Literary Fiction*. Pennsylvania 1994.

Barth, K. *Church Dogmatics: The Doctrine of Reconciliation* IV/1. Tr. G.W. Bromiley. Edinburgh: T. & T. Clark, 1956.

Baudler, G. *God and Violence: The Christian Experience of God in Dialogue with Myths and Other Religions*. Tr. F.C. Lochner. Springfield, IL: Templetgate Publishers, 1992.

Baumann, U. *Erbsünde? Ihr traditionelles Verständnis in der Krise heutiger Theologie* (ÖF.S 2). Freiburg i. Br. 1970.

Beardsley, T. 'Out of food?', *Scientific American* 274/4 (April 1996) 17–18.

Beck, U. *Democracy without Enemies.* Tr. Mark Ritter. Cambridge, UK: Polity Press; Malden, MA: Blackwell, 1998.

Blank, J. Krisis: *Untersuchungen zur johanneischen Christologie und Eschatologie.* Freiburg i. Br. 1964.

Blondel, M. *Die Aktion [1893]: Versuch einer Kritik des Lebens und einer Wissenschaft der Praktik.* Tr. R. Scherer. Freiburg i. Br. 1965.

Boberski, H. *Das Engelwerk: Ein Geheimbund in der katholischen Kirche?* Salzburg 1990.

Bresch, C. *Zwischenstufe Leben: Evolution ohne Ziel?* Fischer-Tb 1280. Frankfurt a. M. 1979.

Büchele, H. 'Jesus und die Öffentlichkeit', *TQ* 165 (1985) 14–28.

Büchele, H. *Sehnsucht nach der Schönen neuen Welt.* Thaur 1993.

Bultmann, R. 'New Testament and Mythology', in *Kerygma and Myth*, 1–44.

Burkert, W. *Homo Necans: The Anthropology of Ancient Greek Sacrificial Ritual and Myth.* Translated by Peter Bing. New York: Walter de Gruyter, 1983.

Byne, W. 'The Biological Evidence Challenged', *Scientific American* 270/5 (May 1994) 26–31.

Capecchi, M.R. 'Targeted Gene Replacement: Researchers can now create mice bearing any chosen mutations in any known gene,' *Scientific American* 270 (1994) 34–41.

Chaos in the Humanities, ed. P. Brady. Knoxville (USA) 1995.

Christus bezeugen (Festschrift W. Trilling), ed K. Kertelge, et al. Freiburg i. Br. 1990.

Colby, S. *Blood sacrifice and cultural evolution in the late preclassic Mesoamerican Southern Pacific Coast and adjacent Highlands.* Los Angeles. University of California / Diss. 1991.

Congar, Y.-M. 'La personne ›Eglise‹', *RThom* 79 (1971) 613–640.

Damasio, H., et al. 'The Return of Phineas Gage: Clues About the Brain from the Skull of a Famous Patient', *Science* 264 (1994) 1102–1105.

Dawkins, R. *The Selfish Gene.* Oxford 1976.

Delumeau, J. *Le péché et la peur: La culpabilisation en Occident [XIIIe- XVIIIe siècles].* Paris 1983.

Demokratiefähigkeit: Jahrbuch Politische Theologie 1 (1996), ed. J. Manemann. Münster 1995.

Denksysteme, Theorien- und Methodenprobleme aus interdiszi-plinärer Sicht, ed. H. Reinalter. Interdisziplinäre Forschung 5. Thaur 1997.

Denzinger, H. Enchiridion symbolorum definitionum et decla-rationum de rebus fidei et morum: Kompendium der Glaubensbekenntnisse und kirchlichen Lehrentscheidungen. Griechisch/Lateinisch – Deutsch, ed. P. Hünermann. Freiburg im Br.: Herder, 1997.

Donald, M. *Origins of the Modern Mind: Three Stages in the Evolution of Culture and Cognition.* Cambridge/USA 1991.

Dostoevsky, F. *The Brothers Karamazov.* Tr. Constance Garnett. Modern Library Series. New York: Random House Modern Library, 1996.

Dostoevsky, F. *Great Short Works of Dostoevsky.* Tr. D. Magarshack. New York: Harper and Row, 1968.

Dramatische Erlösungslehre: Ein Symposion, ed. J. Niewiadomski and W. Palaver. ITS 38. Innsbruck 1992.

Drewermann, E. *Strukturen des Bösen: Die jahwistische Urgeschichte in exegetischer, psychoanalytischer und philosophis-cher Sicht*, Teil 1: *Die jahwistische Urgeschichte in exegetischer Sicht*; Teil 2: *Die jahwistische Urgeschichte in psychoanalytischer Sicht*; Teil 3: *Die jahwistische Urgeschichte in philosophischer Sicht.* PaThSt 4–6. Paderborn 1977–78.

Drewermann, E. *Tiefenpsychologie und Exegese*, Bd. 1: *Die Wahrheit der Formen. Traum, Mythos, Märchen, Sage und Legende.* Olten 1984.

Dubarle, A.M. *Perspectives Theologiques.* Paris 1983.

Duff, P. and Hallmann, J. 'Murder in the Garden? The Envy of the Gods in Genesis 2 and 3', *Contagion: Journal of Violence, Mimesis, and Culture* 3 (1996) 183–200.

Duffy, S.J. 'Our Hearts of Darkness: Original Sin Revisited', *ThSt* 49 (1988) 597–622.

Dumouchel, P. (ed.), *Violence and Truth: On the Work of René Girard*, London, 1988.

Dupuy, J.- P. *Ordres et Désordres: Enquête sur un nouveau para-digme.* Paris 1982.

Dupuy, J.- P. *La panique.* Paris 1991.

Dupuy, J.- P. 'The Self-Deconstruction of the Liberal Order', *Contagion: Journal of Violence, Mimesis, and Culture* 2 (1995) 1–16.

Dupuy, J.-P. 'Tangled Hierarchies: Self- Reference in Philoso-phy, Anthropology and Critical Theory', *Comparative Criticism* 12 (1990) 105–123.

Dürrenmatt, F. *Theaterschriften und Reden*, ed. E. Brock-Sulzer. Zürich 1966.

Duve, Ch. de. 'The Birth of Complex Cells', *Scientific American* 274 (1996) 38–45.

Enzensberger, M. *Aussichten auf den Bürgerkrieg*. Frankfurt a.M. 1993.

Erwin, D. 'The Mother of Mass Extinctions', *Scientific American* 275 (1996) 56–62.

Evolution: Eine Kontroverse, ed. G. Haszprunar and R. Schwager. Interdisziplinäre Forschungen 2. Thaur 1994.

Fessard, G. ' L'Histoire et ses trois niveaux d'historicité', *Sciences écclesiastiques* 18 (1966) 329–357.

Fraine, J. de. *Adam et son lignage: Etudes sur la notion de ›personalité corporative‹ la Bible*. Bruges 1959.

Freud, S. *Moses and Monotheism*. Tr. Katherine Jones. New York: Vintage Books, 1967.

Galleni, L. 'How Does the Teilhardian Vision of Evolution Compare with Contemporary Theories?', *Zygon* 30/1 (1995) 25–45.

Gay, P. *Kult der Gewalt: Aggression im bürgerlichen Zeitalter*. Tr. U. Enderwitz, et al. München 1996.

Girard, R. *Deceit, Desire, and the Novel*. Baltimore: Johns Hopkins University Press, 1965.

Girard, R. *»To double business bound«: Essays on Literature, Mimesis and Anthropology*. Baltimore 1978.

Girard, R. *Job, the Victim of His People*. Tr. Yvonne Freccero. London: Athlone Press, 1987.

Girard, R. *Quand ces choses commenceront* ... Entretiens avec M. Treguer. Paris 1994.

Girard, R. *The Scapegoat*. Tr. Yvonne Freccero. London: Athlone Press, 1986.

Girard, R. *Shakespeare: A Theater of Envy*. New York: Oxford University Press, 1991.

Girard, R. *Things Hidden since the Foundation of the World*. Researches undertaken in collaboration with J.- M. Oughourlian et G. Lefort. Tr. St. Bann and M. Metteer. Stanford: Stanford University Press, 1987.

Girard, R. *Violence and The Sacred*. Tr. P. Gregory. Baltimore: Johns Hopkins University Press, 1977.

Goodall, J. *The Chimpanzees of Gombe: Patterns of Behavior*. Cambridge (USA) 1986.

Gräßer, E. 'Das Seufzen der Kreatur (Röm 8,19–22): Auf der Suche nach einer ›biblischen Tierschutzethik‹', *JBTh* 5 (1990) 93–117.

Haag, E. 'Die Ursünde und das Erbe der Gewalt im Licht der biblischen Urgeschichte', *TrThZ* 98 (1989) 21–38.

Habermas, J. *A Berlin Republic: Writings on Germany.* Tr. Steven Rendall. Intro. By Peter Uwe Hohendahl. Lincoln: University of Nebraska Press, 1997.

Hamerton-Kelly, R.G. *Sacred Violence: Paul's Hermeneutic of the Cross.* Minneapolis 1992.

Hauke, M. *Heilsverlust in Adam: Stationen griechischer Erbsünden-lehre: Irenäus – Origenes – Kappadozier.* KKTS 58. Paderborn 1993.

Heiler, F. *Die Frau in den Religionen der Menschheit.* TBT. Berlin 1976.

Die Herausforderung der Evolutionsbiologie, ed. H. Meier. München ²1989.

Herodotus. *Historien* I/II. Griechisch – Deutsch. Tr. F. Feix. Tusculum Bücherei. München 1963.

Herzog, M. 'Religionstheorie und Theologie René Girards', *KuD* 38 (1992) 105–137.

Hoping, H. *Freiheit im Widerspruch: Eine Untersuchung zur Erbsündenlehre im Ausgang von Immanuel Kant.* ITS 30. Innsbruck 1990.

Horkheimer, M. *Die Sehnsucht nach dem ganz Anderen.* Ein Inter-view mit Kommentar von H. Gumnior. Stundenbücher 97. Hamburg 1970.

Horvath, T. *Eternity and Eternal Life: Speculative Theology and Science in Discourse.* Waterloo (Canada) 1993.

Irenäus. 'Against Heresies,' in *The Apostolic Fathers with Justin Martur and Irenaeus,* ed. A. Cleveland Coxe. Peabody, MA: Hendrickson Publishers, 1995.

Jeismann, M. *Das Vaterland der Feinde: Studien zum nationalen Feindbegriff und Selbstverständnis in Deutschland und Frankreich 1792–1918.* Stuttgart 1992.

Kertelge, K. 'Adam und Christus: Die Sünde Adams im Lichte der Erlösungstat Christi nach Röm 5,12–21', in *Anfänge der Christologie,* 141–153.

Kerygma and Myth by Rudolf Bultmann and Five Critics. Rev. ed. of translation by Reginald Fuller, ed. Barthsch, H.W. New York: Harper, 1961.

Kierkegaard, S. 'Repetition', in idem, *Fear and Trembling/Repeti-tion,* Kierkegaard's Writings VI, ed. and tr. H. and E. Hong. Princeton: Princeton University Press, 1983.

Koltermann, R. *Grundzüge der modernen Naturphilosophie: Ein kritischer Gesamtentwurf.* Frankfurt a. M. 1994.

Kreiner, A. *Ende der Wahrheit? Zum Wahrheitsverständnis in Philosophie und Theologie.* Freiburg i. Br. 1992.

Kufulu Mandunu, J. *Das ›Kindoki‹ im Licht der Sündenbocktheologie: Versuch einer christlichen Bewältigung des Hexenglaubens in Schwarz-Afrika.* Frankfurt a. M. 1992.

Laak, D. van. *Gespräche in der Sicherheit des Schweigens: Carl Schmitt in der politischen Geistesgeschichte der frühen Bundesrepublik.* Berlin 1993.

Lanczkowski, G. *Die Religionen der Azteken, Maya und Inka.* Darmstadt 1989.

Lange, U.P. 'Die dreifache, sich steigernde Offensive Satans, des 'Fürsten dieser Welt', gegen die Kirche', *Una Voce Korrespondenz* 15 (1985) 84–87.

Latour, B. *We Have Never Been Modern.* Tr. C. Poerter. New York/London: Harverster Wheatsheaf, 1993.

LeDoux, J.E., 'Emotion, Memory and the Brain', *Scientific American* 270 (1994) 32–39.

Le Fanu, J. 'Doubts about Darwinism', *The Tablet*, March 2, 1996, 290–291

LeVay, S. and Hamer, D.H. 'Evidence for a Biological Influence in Male Homosexuality,' *Scientific American* 270/5 (May 1994) 20–25.

Lévinas, E. *Otherwise than Being or Beyond Essence.* Tr. A. Lingis. Dordrecht/Boston/London: Kluwer Academic, 1991.

Lévinas, E. *Outside the Subject.* Tr. M. Smith. Stanford: Stanford University Press, 1994.

Lévinas, E. *On Thinking of the Other 'entre nous'.* Tr. M. Smith and B. Harshav. London: Athlone Press, 1998.

Liessmann, K. P. 'Die Technik als Subjekt der Geschichte', in *Wissenschaft und Verantwortlichkeit 1996,* 83–97.

Ligier, L. *Péché d'Adam et péché du monde: Bible – Kippur – Eucharistie* (2 vole). Paris 1960/61.

Lindsey, H. *The Late Great Planet Earth,* with C.C. Carlson. Grand Rapids: Zondervan, 1970.

Linke, D.B. 'Die dritte kopernikanische Wende: Transplantationsmedizin und personale Identität.', *Ethica* 1 (1993) 53–64.

Lohfink, N., et al. *Zum Problem der Erbsünde: Theologische und philosophische Versuche.* Essen 1981.

Lorenz, K. *Die acht Todsünden der zivilisierten Menschheit.* München ²²1990.

Lorenz, K. *Behind the Mirror: A Search for a Natural History of Human Knowledge.* Tr. R. Taylor. London: Methuen, 1977.

Luhmann, N. *Ecological Communication.* Tr. J. Bednarz. Cambridge: Polity, 1989.

Margulis, L. and Sagan, D. *Origins of Sex: Three Billion Years of Genetic Recombination.* New Haven ²1990.

Marsch, M. *Gottes Wege: Heilung durch den Glauben.* Graz 1994.

Martelet, G. *Libre réponse à un scandale: La faute originelle, la souffrance et la mort (Théologies).* Paris ³1987.

Meier, Ch. *The Greek Discovery of Politics.* Tr. David McLintock. Cambridge, MA: Harvard University Press, 1990.

Meyer, P. *Evolution und Gewalt: Ansätze zu einer bio-soziologischen Synthese.* Berlin 1981.

Metz, J. B. 'Monotheismus und Demokratie: Über Religion und Politik auf dem Boden der Moderne', in *Demokratiefähigkeit,* 39–52.

Mühlen, H. *Una mystica persona. Die Kirche als das Mysterium der Identität des Heiligen Geistes in Christus und den Christen: Eine Person in vielen Personen.* München 1964.

Mutschler, H.-D. 'Die Welterklärung der Physik und die Lebenswelt des Menschen,' in *Urknall oder Schöpfung?,* 43–62.

Niethammer, L. *Posthistoire: Has History Come to an End?* Tr. Patrick Camiller. New York: Verso, 1992.

Nietzsche, F. *Thus Spoke Zarathustra.* Tr. R.J. Hollingdale. New York/London: Penguin, 1969.

Nietzsche, F. *Werke,* 3 vols., ed. K. Schlechta. München 1966.

Oberforcher, R. *Die Flutprologe als Kompositionsschlüssel der biblischen Urgeschichte: Ein Beitrag zur Redaktionskritik.* ITS 8. Innsbruck 1981.

Oughourlian, J.-M. *The Puppet of Desire: The Psychology of Hysteria, Possession, and Hypnosis.* Tr. and Introd. E. Webb. Stanford: Stanford University Press, 1991.

Overhage, P. and Rahner, K. *Das Problem der Hominisation: Über den biologischen Ursprung des Menschen.* QD 12/13. Freiburg i.Br. 1961.

Palaver, W. 'Das Arkanum in der Politik: Carl Schmitts Verteidigung der Geheimpolitik', *ThPQ* 144 (1996) 152–167.

Palaver, W. 'Carl Schmitt on Nomos and Space', *Telos* 106 (1996).

Palaver, W. 'Eine doppelte Lektüre der ›Politischen Theologie‹ Carl Schmitts: Zur Rolle der Theologie im interdisziplinären Dialog', in *Denksysteme, Theorien- und Methodenprobleme,* 61–81.

Palaver, W. 'Foundational Violence and Hannah Arendt's Political Philosophy', *Paragrana* 4 (1995) 166–176.

Palaver, W. 'A Girardian Reading of Schmitt's Political Theology', *Telos* 93 (1992) 43–68.

Palaver, W. *Die mythischen Quellen des Politischen: Carl Schmitts Freund-Feind-Theorie*. Beiträge zur Friedensethik 27. Stuttgart: Kohlhammer, 1998.

Palaver, W. 'Order out of Chaos in the Theories of Carl Schmitt and René Girard', in *Chaos in the Humanities*, 87–106.

Palaver, W. 'Die Politische Theologie des Großinquisitors: Bemerkungen zu Heinrich Meiers Buch 'Die Lehre Carl Schmitts'', *ZKTh* 118 (1996) 36–49.

Palaver, W. 'Schmitt's Critique of Liberalism', *Telos* 102 (1995) 43–71.

Pannenberg, W. *Systematic Theology*, Vol. 2. Tr. G. Bromiley. Edinburgh: T. & T. Clark, 1994.

Philo of Alexandria. 'On the Account of the World's Creation Given by Moses. Nr. 16:129–135', in idem, *Works* 1. Tr. F.H. Colson. Cambridge, MA: Harvard University Press, 1949.

Poliakov, L. *La causalité diabolique*, Vol.1: *Essai sur l'origine des persécutions*. Paris 1980; vol. 2: *Du joug mongol à la victoire de Lénine*. Paris 1985.

Poliakov, L. *The History of Anti-Semitism*, 4 vols. Philadelphia: University of Pennsylvania Press, 2003.

Polkinghorne, J. 'The Nature of Physical Reality', *Zygon* 26 (1991) 221–236.

Pöltner, G. 'Evolutionäre Erkenntnislehre,' in *Evolution: Eine Kontroverse*, 133–146.

Pottier, B. 'Interpréter le péché originel sur les traces de G. Fessard', *NRT* 111 (1989) 801–823.

Rad, G. von. *Old Testament Theology*, vol. 1: *The Theology of Israel's Traditions*. Tr. D.M.G. Stalker. New York: Harper and Row, 1962.

Rahner, K. 'On Angels', in idem, *Theological Investigations* XIX (Faith and Ministry). Tr. E. Quinn. London: Burns & Oates, 1980.

Rahner, K. 'Christology within an Evolutionary View of the World', in idem, *Theological Investigations* V. Tr. K.H. Kruger. Baltimore: Helicon Press, 1966.

Rahner, K. 'The Experiment with Man', in idem, *Theological Investigations* IX. Tr. G. Harrison. London: Darton, Longman & Todd, 1972.

Rahner, K. *Foundations of Christian Faith: An Introduction to the Idea of Christianity*. Tr. W. Dych. London: Darton Longman & Todd, 1978.

Rahner, K. *Hominisation: The Evolutionary Origin of Man as a Theological Problem*. Tr. W.T. O'Hara. London: Burns & Oates, 1965.

Rahner, K. *Schriften zur Theologie*, 16 vols. Einsiedeln/Zürich 1954–1984.

Rahner, K. 'The Sin of Adam', in idem, *Theological Investigations* XI. Tr. W. Dych. London: Darton Longman & Todd, 1978.

Rahner, K. *Spirit in the World*. Translated by W. Dych. London: Sheed and Ward, 1979.

Rahner, K. 'Theology of Freedom', in idem, *Theological Investigations* VI. Tr. K.-H. and B. Kruger. New York: Crossroad, 1969.

Rainer, M. J. 'Carl Schmitt und Johann Baptist Metz in fremder Nähe? Bemerkungen zu zwei Leitkonzepten politischer Theologie im 20. Jahrhundert', in *Demokratiefähigkeit*, 82–106.

Ricoeur, P. *The Symbolism of Evil*. Tr. E. Buchanan. New York: Harper and Row, 1967.

Rorty, R. *Contingency, Irony, and Solidarity*. Cambridge and New York: Cambridge University Press, 1989.

Runggaldier, E. *Was sind Handlungen? Eine philosophische Auseinandersetzung mit dem Naturalismus*. MPhS. N.F. 12. Stuttgart 1996.

Schmitt, C. *The Concept of the Political*. Tr., Introd., and Notes G. Schwab. Comments by L. Strauss. New Brunswick: Rutgers University Press, 1976..

Schmitt, C. *Politische Theologie II: Die Legende von der Erledigung jeder Politischen Theologie*. Berlin 1970.

Schmitz-Moormann, K. *Die Erbsünde: Überholte Vorstellung – Bleibender Glaube*. Olten et al 1969.

Schnackenburg, R. *The Gospel according to St. John*, Vol. 2. Tr. C. Hastings. New York: Seabury, 1980.

Schneider, R. *Winter in Wien: Aus meinen Notizbüchern 1957–58*. Herder Bücherei 142. Freiburg i. Br. 1963.

Schönborn, Ch. et al. *Zur kirchlichen Erbsündenlehre: Stellungnahmen zu einer brennenden Frage*. Kriterien 87. Einsiedeln 1991.

Schwager, R. et al, *Dramatische Theologie als Forschungsprogramm*. ZKTh 118 (1996) 317–344. [English online edition: *Dramatic Theology as a Research Program*, available at: http://theol.uibk.ac.at/rgkw/xtext/research-0.html]

Schwager, R. 'Hörer des Wortes: Eine empirische Anthropologie für die Theologie?', *ZKTh* 114 (1992) 1–23.

Schwager, R. *Jesus in the Drama of Salvation: Toward a Biblical Doctrine of Redemption.* Tr. J. Williams and P. Haddon. New York: Crossroad, 1999.

Schwager, R. *Must There Be Scapegoats? Violence and Redemption in the Bible.* Tr. M.L. Assad. New York: Crossroad, 2000.

Schwager, R. 'Neues und Altes zur Lehre von der Erbsünde', *ZKTh* 116 (1994) 1–29 [now the first chapter of *Banished from Eden*].

Schwager, R. 'Der vom Himmel gefallene Satan: Wer oder was ist der Teufel?', *ThG* 35 (1992) 255–264.

Schwager, R. *Der wunderbare Tausch: Zur Geschichte und Deutung der Erlösungslehre.* München 1986.

Sharpin, S. and Schaffer, S. *Leviathan and the Air-Pump: Hobbes, Boyle und the Experimental Life.* Princeton 1985.

Sitte, P. 'Evolution – Fakten, Faktoren, Konzepte, Konsequenzen,' in *Evolution. Eine Herausforderung,* 9–28.

Sobrino, J. *Sterben muß, wer an Götzen rührt.* Fribourg 1990.

Spaemann, R. 'Über einige Schwierigkeiten mit der Erbsündenlehre,' in Schönborn, Ch. *Zur kirchlichen Erbsündenlehre,* 41–66.

Spee, F. von. *Cautio criminalis, or a Book on Witch Trials.* Tr. M. Hellyer. *Charlottesville: University Press of Virginia* 2003.

Stocker, J. *Prophezeiungen über bevorstehende Ereignisse: Der Dritte Weltkrieg und was danach kommt.* St Andrä-Wördern ⁷1991.

Teilhard de Chardin. *Activation of Energy.* Tr. R. Hague. London: Collins, 1970.

Teilhard de Chardin. *Christianity and Evolution.* Tr. R. Hague. London: Collins, 1971.

Teilhard de Chardin. *The Divine Milieu.* San Francisco: Harper-Collins Perennial Classics, 2001.

Teilhard de Chardin. *The Human Phenomenon.* Tr. S. Appleton-Weber. Brighton: Sussex Academic Press, 2003.

Thomas Aquinas. *Summa Theologiae,* Vol. 13. Tr, Introd., notes E. Hill. London: Eyre & Spottiswood; New York: McGraw-Hill Books, 1964.

Thomas Aquinas. *Summa Theologiae,* Vol. 15. Tr., Introd., Notes M.J. Charlesworth. London: Eyre & Spottiswood; New York: McGraw-Hill Books, 1970.

Tierney, P. *Zu Ehren der Götter: Menschenopfer in den Anden.* Tr. D. Mrkowatschki. München 1989.

Tipler, F. *Die Physik der Unsterblichkeit: Moderne Kosmologie, Gott und die Auferstehung der Toten.* Tr. I. Leipold. München ²1994.

Tomatis, A. '"Écouter, c'est se converti": Interview du Docteur Alfred Tomatis'. *Sources Vives* 30 (13, rue des Barres, 75004 Paris), 78–88.

Tomatis, A. *La nuit utérine.* Paris: Stock ³1993.

Tomatis, A. *Neuf mois au Paradis: Histoires de la vie prénatale.* Avec la collaboration de L. Sellin. Paris 1989.

Tomatis, A. *L'Oreille et la vie: Itinéraire d'une recherche sur l'audition, la langue et la communication.* Paris ²1990.

Tomatis, A. *L'Oreille et la voix.* Dessins de P. Guillaume et V. Simon. Paris 1987.

Understandig Origins: Contemporary Views on the Origin of Life, Mind and Society, ed. F. Varela, et al. Boston Studies in the Philosophy of Science 130. Dordrecht 1992.

Urknall oder Schöpfung?, ed. W. Gräb. Gütersloh 1995.

Die verdrängte Freiheit: Fundamentalismus in den Kirchen, ed. H. Kochanek. Freiburg i. Br. 1991.

Verweyen, H. *Gottes letztes Wort: Grundriß der Fundamentaltheologie.* Düsseldorf 1991.

Violence and Truth: On the Work of René Girard, ed. P. Dumouchel. London 1988.

Vogel, Ch. *Vom Töten zum Mord: Das wirklich Böse in der Evolutionsgeschichte.* München 1989.

Voland, E. *Grundriß der Soziobiologie.* Uni-Taschenbücher 1730. Stuttgart 1993.

Völker, W. *Maximus Confessor als Meister des geistlichen Lebens.* Wiesbaden 1965.

Waal, F. de. *Peacemaking among Primates.* Cambridge/Mass: Harvard University Press, 1989.

Walter, N. 'Gottes Zorn und das ›Harren der Kreatur‹', in *Christus bezeugen,* 218–226.

Wege der Totalitarismus-Forschung, ed. B. Seidel and S. Jenkner. WdF 140. Darmstadt 1968.

Wiedenhofer, S. 'Zum gegenwärtigen Stand der Erbsündentheologie', *ThRv* 83 (1987) 353–370.

Wiedenhofer, S. 'Hauptformen gegenwärtiger Erbsündentheologie', *IkZ* 20 (1991) 315–328.

Wieser, W. 'Die Evolution hat viele Gesichter – und jedes sieht dich,' in *Evolution: Eine Kontroverse,* 29–55.

Wilckens, U. *Der Brief an die Römer,* Bd. 2: Röm 6–11. EKK. Zürich 1980.

Williams, J. G. *The Bible, Violence and the Sacred: Liberation from the Myth of Sanctioned Violence*. San Francisco 1991.

Winkler, E.-M. 'Stufen der Hominisation', in *Evolution: Eine Kontroverse*, 95–106.

Wissenschaft und Verantwortlichkeit 1996: Die Wissenschaft – eine Gefahr für die Welt?, ed. H. Barta, et al. Wien 1996.

Index of Subjects

Index of Names